This book is for all the supporters and contributors to the events of 2008 and 2012, and to those who continue in our struggle. Your generosity and your dedication to the cause of peace and liberty is a true inspiration.

also by Ron Paul:

The Revolution at Ten Years

by Ron Paul

Foreword by Llewellyn H. Rockwell, Jr.

ISBN: 978-0-9964265-5-8

cover photo: Gage Skidmore

design/production by Cynthia Fedler

Ron Paul Institute
FOR PEACE AND PROSPERITY
WWW.RONPAULINSTITUTE.ORG
833 W. Plantation Dr. ✦ Clute, TX 77531

Contents

Foreword

What is the Revolution ten years ago that Ron Paul's book aims to assess? He tells us, "On December 16, 2007, the spark of liberty would ignite with the modern-day Tea Party 'Revolution.' On that day, thousands of people used the 234th anniversary of the original Boston Tea Party to celebrate the ideas of freedom. Americans were letting it be known that they had had enough! Change was finally in the air."

The Tea Party soon was co-opted by the Republican political establishment, but a much more significant movement kept its principles intact. This was the movement led by the heroic Ron Paul himself, and his new book makes clear why he has inspired millions.

Ron Paul served in Congress for many years, ranging from the 1970s to 2013, and he quickly became known as freedom's foremost advocate. He defended the gold standard, called for the abolition of the Fed, opposed government regulations that interfere with the free market, and resolutely challenged war and militarism.

During his three campaigns for president, people all over America and the world became aware of his views. He appealed especially to young people, and his theme of "End the Fed" resonated across university campuses all over the country. In 2008 and 2012, he directly confronted warmongers like John McCain and Mitt Romney. Although the Republican establishment used dirty tricks to take away his votes, he became a national and international presence that no one could ignore.

For Ron Paul, recent history is a struggle between liberty and tyranny. "While the concept of liberty remained in its infancy for thousands of years, something amazing happened in the 18th century. The importance of the individual and his inherent liberty was recognized and defined. This occurred most notably in America and in other Western countries. This recognition led to the explosion of human progress from which we continue to benefit to this very day. It proved to be the most important development for all of mankind. The preparation of a habitable place for the human race to thrive took billions of years. The amazing progress of mankind in comparison has been accomplished in a flash of time."

America was founded on a philosophy of freedom. "A tremendous victory was achieved in America from 1776 to 1787. The Declaration of Independence clearly recognized the principle of natural rights and the importance of the individual over the collective."

Unfortunately, the Progressive Movement revolted against freedom, and this has led to economic planning and war since the late nineteenth century. "Ignorance and barbarism returned with a vengeance. The pushback was from a body of ideas known as 'progressivism.' This opposition would usher in the deadliest and most murderous governments in the history of mankind. The 20th century featured the response of power to the ideas of liberty. Communism, socialism, and fascism would ravage the Earth."

Ron Paul has devoted his life to the battle against the anti-freedom movement. He identifies with clinical precision the tactics used by the leviathan state. Economic planning ranks among the most important of these. "Government economic planning is considered by most university pro-fessors of economics to be superior to voluntary individual planning. Our college students have been taught for decades that it is possible to steer away from the extreme government planning of socialism, fascism, and communism to find a happy medium with Keynesian-type interventionism."

To finance the State's efforts to suppress liberty through planning, the Federal Reserve System has played a vital role. "An interventionist state needs a financier, and that is where the Federal Reserve comes in. Taxation alone is not enough to fund a leviathan state. The ability to create new money out of thin air acts as the beating heart of big government."

With the vast financial resources made available by the Fed, the State has followed a policy of war and militarism. This policy has led to disaster after disaster. "The military-in-dustrial complex always has a never-ending series of mon-sters that we need to destroy. There is always a new Hitler ready to be displayed on every magazine cover as the next target. Even though there is no threat of anyone invading America in an effort to take it over, Americans are kept in a perpetual state of fear. . . Fear works. Decade after decade, the military-industrial-complex simply recycles the same tac-tics to keep fear and war alive."

Ron Paul will not compromise. He calls for a complete end to our militaristic foreign policy and a turn to peace and non-intervention. "Whether government tries to run our lives at home, or attempts to 'remake' people in other countries across the world, the inevitable result is misery. This process has given a severe and shocking blow to Western civilization, which was built on the opposite principles."

Readers of this book will gain a clear perspective on the meaning of history. Ron Paul has carefully studied the works of Ludwig von Mises and Murray Rothbard. This, combined with his courage and devotion to freedom, has made him the foremost leader in the struggle against the cultural Marxists, the radical environmentalists, the "deep state," and all other enemies of freedom.

Although "skepticism about the human condition improving in the near future is justified," Ron Paul remarks, "my optimism remains. There is no reason to accept the premise that solutions to these many problems are not available to us. "Readers of The Revolution at Ten Tears will be inspired for the difficult days of struggle ahead.

—Llewellyn H. Rockwell, Jr.,
founder and chairman, Ludwig von Mises Institute

1 The Rise of Liberty

The libertarian philosophy, comparatively speaking, is a very new idea. It still has a long way to go with a very bright future. The advance of civilization depends on its success.

Fortunately, the era of excessive government intrusion that has taken place over the past hundred years is now coming to an end. Government dominance in everyday life has created many significant problems for average people all over the world. Yet, the ideas of liberty, though rarely practiced by any single government, continue to advance.

The history of mankind is remarkably short. Our solar system—the earth, moon, planets, and our sun—is estimated to be about 4.5 billion years old. Some people claim that there is evidence of human existence for as long as 200,000 years of prehistory—a period from which there are no written records, since the process of writing had not yet been discovered.

Civilization is considered to be approximately 6,000 years old, which coincides with the record-keeping that came with the development of writing.

When we look at the relatively minuscule amount of time that has been spent thinking about liberty, we find that it's a very new, hardly touched-upon phenomenon that has ignited amazing improvements around the world.

While the concept of liberty remained in its infancy for thousands of years, something amazing happened in the 18th century. The importance of the individual and his inherent liberty was recognized and defined. This occurred most notably in America and in other Western countries. This recognition led to the explosion of human progress from which we continue to benefit to this very day. It proved to be the most important development for all of mankind.

The preparation of a habitable place for the human race to thrive took billions of years. The amazing progress of mankind in comparison has been accomplished in a flash of time.

The authority of one person to control others with force became an important issue for all societies. Development of a full understanding of the morality of liberty has been slow, but the benefits provided in the last 250 years have been remarkable. Considering the actual time involved, it amounts to a very small drop, not in the bucket, but in the ocean!

Let's take a brief look at a few significant events that preceded the explosion of human progress in the 18th century.

Among the earliest known legal codes is the Hammurabi Code. It is thought to have been written in Babylon in Mesopotamia in around 1760 BC or 3,700 years ago. The code dealt with proper and decent behavior of citizens and the responsibility of the king to dispense justice. It covered the concept of good versus evil, proper governing power, and just punishments for lawbreaking.

The Hammurabi Code was a primitive set of laws. But, it was significant in its intent. It was recognized that if judges did not act fairly, they would suffer a penalty. Judges who erred were fined and removed from their positions. The intent was to clarify the people's understanding of their "rights" and what prohibitions were placed on their activities.

Interestingly, the code even recognized the presumption of innocence and that the accused had a right to provide evidence on his behalf. It is too bad our current government agencies—especially the IRS—have not been forced to grant the same protection to Americans that people were provided with 3,700 years ago.

The Hammurabi Code, though far from perfect, did recognize other basic principles respecting individual rights and prescribed penalties for slander, theft, violation of contracts, and personal liability in cases of injury.

Hammurabi's laws set standards for some of our laws today. Unfortunately, we have forgotten some of the wisdom that existed that long ago, when these laws were first written.

Several hundred years after the Hammurabi Code was written, another code for personal conduct and behavior was used for the basis of law. It was introduced to mankind when Moses delivered the Ten Commandments to the Jewish people. Both the Hammurabi Code and the Ten Commandments were connected to religious beliefs. Parts of the Ten Commandments influenced the writing of laws that reflect an understanding of personal rights and have persisted to this day.

The Ten Commandments, originated in Judaism, were accepted by Christianity 2000 years ago and were essentially repeated in the early 7th century in the Quran. Obviously, the theology among the three great religions varies, but the significance of what was important for writing man's laws for maintaining a stable society was clear. When it came to respect for life and property, it meant keeping your word, no theft, no lying or false testimony, no murder, and no wrongful desire for someone else's property. Simply put, a civilized society should be made up of people who do not lie, steal, cheat, or murder.

Portions of the Old Testament—the parts that emphasize wise judges over the militarism of kings, along with the Christian emphasis on individualism and personal responsibility for one's actions, strongly influenced the advancement of the human race. They encouraged developing a society that cherishes liberty over authoritarianism and that emphasizes moral and religious principles.

Eight hundred years ago, another major advancement was made in the rise of liberty. The adopting of the Magna Carta continued the efforts of the Hammurabi Code and the Ten Commandments.

In 1215 in England, a group of barons revolted against King John. The barons had grievances with taxation and foreign entanglements. The king was forced to sign the Magna Carta. The Magna Carta codified the principle of habeas corpus and clearly stated that the king was no longer above the law.

Next, a tremendous victory was achieved in America from 1776 to 1787. The Declaration of Independence clearly recognized the principle of natural rights and the importance of the individual over the collective. The US Constitution that followed was intended to place strict controls on government power.

The growing recognition and understanding of individual liberty ushered in the Industrial Revolution in the mid-18th century through the mid-19th century. With the repeal of Great Britain's tariff-imposing Corn Laws in 1846, free trade was established. There was also movement toward free trade in other parts of the world in the 19th century, including in America.

The Industrial Revolution improved the living conditions of the masses, who prior to it lived lives that were brutish and short. The progress that was made far surpassed the progress of the previous 6,000 years of recorded history, as well as a couple hundred thousand years of prehistory.

In his book *Omnipotent Government,* the great Austrian economist Ludwig von Mises described this general time period as having a "trend toward freedom, the rights of man, and self-determination." Mises continued: "This individualism resulted in the fall of autocratic government, the establishment of democracy, the evolution of capitalism, technical improvements, and an unprecedented rise in standards of living. It substituted enlightenment for old superstitions, scientific methods of research for inveterate prejudices. It was an epoch of great artistic and literary achievements, the age of immortal musicians, painters, writers, and philosophers."

Greater freedom has permitted scientific knowledge and technical advances to improve the living standards of billions of people around the world.

While the rise of liberty had been astounding and quick, a serious pushback confronted it towards the end of the 1800s and continued to have much strength.

Opposition to liberty from those who cherish power was expected. Thomas Jefferson warned in an 1816 letter to John Adams that, "we are destined to be a barrier against the returns of ignorance and barbarism."

Jefferson was correct. Ignorance and barbarism returned with a vengeance. The pushback was from a body of ideas known as "progressivism." This opposition would usher in the deadliest and most murderous governments in the history of mankind.

The 20th century featured the response of power to the ideas of liberty. Communism, socialism, and fascism would ravage the Earth. The technological progress that resulted from the Industrial Revolution would be hijacked by governments to wage wars of a type the world had never seen before. No one would be spared. Countless innocents would die at the hands of these tyrannical states.

Belief in the individual would be discarded. Going forward, the focus was to be on the "the collective" or "the common good." A better world for everyone was promised with a devoted passion. The intellectual classes swallowed the ideas of collectivism and tossed aside the principles of liberty.

For the tyrants, who would define "the common good," the state became the embodiment of their authority. They saw themselves as the definers of truth and law. In many cases they exercised powers much as if they were gods. The people were to be completely subservient to the whims of dictators.

Americans would fall to the ideas of progressivism as well. The year 1913 dealt a swift blow to liberty in the United States. The 16th Amendment was passed, creating the personal income tax. The Federal Reserve Act was also passed, creating a monopolistic central bank in the United States.

During the same time period, America's strong tradition of a noninterventionist foreign policy was tossed aside. A needless and reckless rush into World War I ensued.

The utopian world that the collectivist intellectuals theorized and envisioned did not come to be. Instead of creating a heaven on Earth, they created a living hell.

Most of the thugs who ended up in charge of providing

for the masses lived quite well themselves. But hundreds of millions of their citizens were slaughtered as a result of failed ideas.

The death counts were astonishing, including tens of millions of deaths due to the actions of the governments of Mao Zedong, Joseph Stalin, and Adolf Hitler. When factoring in the other dictators, R. J. Rummel estimated a total of 262 million people were killed in the 20th century. This was in addition to those who died in wars waged by governments.

Ultimately, the fascist and communist murderers' government systems collapsed.

Even in the midst of the 20th century's slaughter, the flame of liberty persisted. For libertarians, Franklin D. Roosevelt's New Deal was more of a "raw deal." It was definitely not a program to resuscitate the Founding Fathers' dream of establishing a free society based on the principles of personal liberty and private property.

As a reaction to FDR, a small but elite group of intellectuals spoke out against the dangerous welfare-warfare state that they saw coming. Though they have been referred to the Old Right, they were essentially libertarians. This group was laying the foundation for libertarian thinking that advanced much in the second half of the 20th century.

One particular individual among those who led the charge in libertarian thinking following World War II was a key influence on me and my desire to be part of this effort. His name was Leonard Read. In order to promote libertarian thinking, Read established a new organization the Foundation for Economic Education (FEE) in 1946. FEE performed a magnificent service by preserving and promoting the ideas of liberty in a time when the country was going in the opposite direction. Read was leading an intellectual awakening, which would be necessary to bring about major political changes.

Read had been influenced by other authors who espoused the ideas of liberty, including Frédéric Bastiat, F.A. Hayek, Henry Hazlitt, Ludwig von Mises, Albert Jay Nock, and Ayn Rand. These writers championed the ideas of liberty despite the fact that the Soviet Union was still in existence and American intellectuals kept expounding the virtues of socialism.

Western intellectuals believed that socialist societies were doing well and would eventually pass the US and Western Europe in prosperity. They could not have been more wrong.

A major blow against the ideas of collectivism was the disappearance of the Soviet Empire. The fall of the Berlin Wall caught the intellectuals by complete surprise. The "utopia" had completely collapsed, without a single shot having to be fired.

Lech Walesa, the leader of Solidarity in Poland recalled in an interview at the 2000 International Achievement Summit: "In the 1970s and in the 1980s, I had conversations with all the powerful people of the world: with presidents, with prime ministers, chancellors and kings, too. None of them believed that there was any chance of us toppling communism before the year 2000. I didn't meet a single person among those people who would believe that was possible. Not a single one in the whole world."

Free-market economists and authors, who understood the principles of private property, sound money, free market prices, and the law of supply and demand, were not surprised at all by the fall of the Soviet Union. For decades they logically explained why the whole Soviet state was a house of cards that would collapse from internal rather than external pressure. Economic law would bring the Soviets down, not nuclear missiles.

Of course, much like today, free-market economists were ignored since power had no use for the truth.

The fall of the Soviet Empire provided a golden opportunity for the United States to dismantle its socialism at home. It also provided the opportunity to bring the troops home from all over the world. After all, the monster that had been propagandized as the world's biggest threat was no longer a threat.

But a turn towards liberty would not be in the cards. Mises Institute Chairman Lew Rockwell recounted at a January of 2000 Mises Institute event how the power elites reacted to the collapse of the Soviet Union: "I recall noticing a distinct lack of jubilance on the part of the ruling class when it woke up one day and found its reliable enemy (the Soviet Union) had ceased to exist."

Governments of the West, who accumulated tremendous powers to battle the Soviet threat, had no interest in giving those powers up.

Instead of capitalizing on the newfound peace, the US and its NATO allies unnecessarily began engaging in conflicts in the Middle East. The killing by governments through war would continue, though at a reduced rate when compared to the killings under Mao, Stalin, and Hitler.

Nevertheless, several million people have died as a consequence of the US led or supported interventions in the Middle East, including invasions, bombings, sanctions, and provocations of civil wars for regime change.

The era of Nazism, fascism, and communism may be over, but a new gang of rulers, who were very anxious to change the image of authoritarianism, merely took their place.

The wrong choices would be made domestically as well. Even after the astronomical collapse of communism, the idea of economic planning by governments continued to be embraced by nations around the world, including the US.

Obviously, the progress of liberty has not been a straight line upwards. Many setbacks have occurred, including over the last 100 years in the United States.

But the upward climb of liberty can continue nevertheless. The "Progressive Era" is coming to an end as government interventionism is failing. There are many reasons to remain optimistic.

The Austrian economist Murray Rothbard wrote in his book *For a New Liberty*, "I am convinced that the dark night of tyranny is ending, and that a new dawn of liberty is now at hand." My presidential campaigns from 2008 and 2012 have also convinced me that there is so much to be optimistic about. The ideas of liberty are still alive and well!

2 The 2007 "R☒☒☒ution"

We are living at the end of the "Progressive Era," which began a little more than 100 years ago. The time period has been dominated by the idea that government has the ability to improve society by using aggressive force. After the last 100-plus years, the results are quite obvious. The idea is just not true; government can do no such thing. Instead, the state has consistently produced the exact opposite outcome.

The American people once had a proud and vehement love for liberty. But it was methodically eroded away by "progressive" ideas about the role of government. Instead of protecting our liberty, as was intended by America's Founding Fathers, the government morphed into a bureaucratic monster at home and an aggressive military empire abroad.

However, on December 16, 2007, the spark of liberty would ignite with the modern-day Tea Party "Revolution." On that day, thousands of people used the 234th anniversary of the original Boston Tea Party to celebrate the ideas of freedom. Americans were letting it be known that they had had enough! Change was finally in the air.

Those who had heard the message let their frustrations with overbearing government be known. They were determined to spread the message of liberty to others.

By 2007, abuse by our own government had far surpassed any abuses by the British government of the 1770s. The outbursts were long overdue.

The demonstrations were accompanied by an Internet fundraising campaign, known as a "money bomb," that produced over $6 million in donations in a single day! It was a record for fundraising on the Internet at that time. And, yet, mainstream media coverage was scarce.

As expected, both the Republican and Democratic Parties dismissed these views of freedom as "extreme" and out of the mainstream.

Despite media indifference, the enthusiastic support for the "Revolution" far exceeded most people's expectations. It would continue for the next four years, producing even greater support and bigger demonstrations for the cause of liberty during my 2012 presidential campaign.

Young people especially recognized the failure of government. Constant attacks on civil liberties, including violations of personal privacy, had become rampant. They recognized that economic policy was based on the silly notion that if the Federal Reserve printed a lot of money and ignored debt as a nuisance, everyone would be better off and our problems would be solved.

Those who understood what liberty is all about also knew that senseless wars in the Middle East do nothing to enhance our national security, while imposing an additional unnecessary financial burden on all Americans.

The people in the large crowds at my campaign events were able to easily reject the "mainstream" when an alternative was offered and defended intellectually.

As encouraging and exciting as these events turned out to

be, the tremendous momentum of the 2007 Tea Party would be sidetracked. Its importance would be diminished by it being co-opted by establishment politicians and the media. The Tea Party essentially became an arm of the Republican Party and has subsequently been usurped by Trumpism. The watered-down version of the Tea Party replacement is no longer ideologically significant today.

But, though the "Revolution" of 2007 is essentially forgotten in a political sense, the ideology that inspired it is very much alive, and the anger and loss of confidence in our current system continues to steadily grow.

If one measures the status of the liberty movement by the current crop of politicians in place, along with the media and universities, it may appear that the movement is nonexistent. But that is just not the case. The defenders of liberty, free markets, and private property are still providing a very strong undercurrent.

It must always be remembered that the importance of ideas will always dwarf the importance of the raw power upon which politicians rely. We need ideological influence as well as political efforts, but, of the two, ideas count much more.

This is true for both good and bad ideas. Bad ideas, when they prevail, are quite dangerous to the lives and liberties of all individuals. The last 100 years provide proof of that. But good ideas, when they are finally embraced, produce a great burst of energy for all of humanity. We can look at the 18th and 19th centuries as a guide.

The electoral process is "owned" by a political monopoly, controlled by Republicans and Democrats. Both fear any effort to diminish their power. They work together in discrediting any opposition to the status quo. Ballot access restrictions, media blackouts, debate exclusions, and efforts by various special interests have all been used to minimize the impact of the ideas of liberty in the American electoral process.

The political progress for libertarians has been slow and tedious, but the intellectual achievements in an educational movement promoting liberty are exceptional.

Today we have a government that constantly lies to us. As more and more people come to realize this, trust in government plummets. Pew Research Center polling over the last ten years found that 70 percent or more of the American people do not trust that the US government will either just about always or most of the time do what is right.

With all the anger and frustration that Americans feel towards the government, the 2016 election became a convenient vehicle for harnessing that energy. Add up the Trump vote, the Sanders vote, the alternative parties vote, and those who refused to participate in what to them appeared to be a charade, and one can see a high degree of discontent exists throughout America.

The recent election was nasty, and strong anti-establishment sentiments were significant and varied. Understanding the 2016 election's relation to the discontent expressed in 2008 to 2012 is important.

There was a major problem this time around. The principal candidates did not offer a philosophic alternative to the status quo. Instead, they upheld the continuation of a military empire abroad and central economic planning at home.

Liberty was not forcefully and consistently offered to the people. In fact, it was virtually unmentioned.

But, whether the ideas of liberty end up getting a fair hearing or not, the consequences of the current system cannot be avoided. After the 2016 election left the status quo largely unchanged, all proponents of and believers in liberty must work diligently to offer the intellectual ammunition that will usher in a new and enlightened era.

It is important to understand that democracy should not be our goal. Democracy is seductive tyranny. It does not ensure protection of minorities or of believers in liberty, and it can promote the dictatorship of the majority.

Americans have accepted democracy at all costs in spite of the Founders' warnings about its danger to a constitutional republic that has the goal of protecting liberty.

Thomas Jefferson wrote in Notes on the State of Virginia that "[a]n elective despotism was not the government we fought for." The "Father of the Constitution" James Madison observed in the Federalist Papers Number 10 that democracies "have ever been spectacles of turbulence and contention, have ever been found incompatible with personal security and the rights of property."

Unfortunately, this wise advice, from individuals who were well aware of political history, has been systematically ignored. Today, the majority is treated as sacrosanct.

Americans feel like the government reflects the will of the people. If they are unhappy, they are instructed to start working on the "next" election to get "their" candidate elected. But nothing changes, no matter who is elected. The same policies of welfare at home and warfare abroad continue without a hitch. Surveillance of every American increases. Privacy and liberty decrease.

Think about this quote for a moment. It is from freelance journalist Gary Allen in his 1971 book *None Dare Call It Conspiracy*: "Millions of Americans are concerned and frustrated over mishappenings in our nation. They feel that something is wrong, drastically wrong." Allen further wrote, "Each new administration, whether it be Republican or Democrat, continues the same basic policies of the previous administration which it had so thoroughly denounced during the election campaign."

That was written 46 years ago, and it still applies to this day! Both Republicans and Democrats are believers in the "progressive" ideology. Both believe that government's use of aggressive force can improve society. The election of 2016 did nothing to change this.

So tinkering with democracy will never provide the answer that we need.

Neither is "populism" the solution to overbearing government. It has been said that populism won in the 2016 election. But populism is not the type of change needed for the "Revolution" and the advancement of human liberty. The problems that we face are structural. As in previous elections, campaign rhetoric offered in 2016 has elicited hope, but we will end up with more of the same.

Traditional populism incorporates protectionism, welfare directed to the poor, more taxes on the rich, and a paper money system where the Congress controls the printing press and the distribution of the money is designed to meet the needs of the poor, especially the farmers.

Emphasizing personal liberty and free trade is not part of the populist platform. Strong nationalism is a vital part of populist thinking.

Even some proponents of libertarianism claim that they too are "populist" and that populism is the only system that can truly boost the economic well-being of the poor and middle class. Libertarianism may be "populistic" in the general sense of helping the poor and middle class, but populism in the specific sense is not libertarianism.

Helping the poor in a libertarian society requires no government force to compel the redistribution of wealth. Instead, help for the poor comes as a natural consequence of liberty, private property, sound money, and voluntary exchanges.

Many pundits now are claiming that the libertarian message has been significantly set back and that the answers to our problems will be found in Bernie Sanders- and Donald Trump-style populism. Politico suggested in the title of a 2017 article that we are seeing "The End of the Libertarian Dream." The author of the Politico article recognized the burst of energy for the libertarian "revolution" related to my 2008 and 2012 presidential campaigns, but proposes that support for the message faded in 2016 due to "fear" generated by "Jihadi John" and ISIS, along with the ascendance of Donald Trump to the presidency.

That fear was created by the war propaganda driven by the media, the military-industrial complex, and the neoconservative influence in favor of imperialism.

When the full results of interventionism's failure become evident, its rejection will usher in the greatest opportunity ever for the message of liberty to offer solutions.

In the meantime, I expect the intellectual influence of libertarian thinkers and the acceptance of the freedom philosophy will continue to grow.

Much like the shock after the fall of the Soviet Union, the end of the Keynesian economic era will be dramatic and shocking to many in government, the media, universities, and world financial markets.

Libertarian options will be seen as an answer to the 100-plus years of bad domestic and foreign policies that have brought us to the brink of an economic and political disaster.

It will be discovered that the current "populism" doesn't provide the answers and is nothing more than political re-adjustment of the existing system of interventionism. With debt growing more than twice as fast as gross domestic product, stagnation and decline will prevail. There is zero chance that total expenditures by the US government will decrease. The creation of new money out of thin air, for which the entire world is dependent, will continue until the final disintegration of the current system occurs.

Libertarianism will offer the options necessary to achieve economic prosperity and peace.

Now let's get a handle on the major challenges that we have before us. The first step is always self-education and understanding. As Lew Rockwell wrote in the book *The Economics of Liberty*: "The obstacles are, of course, immense. But we have a world to win."

3 Economic Central Planning

Because the American homeland was able to escape the physical destruction of two world wars, the US was in the best position when it came time to negotiate peace terms. With manufacturing intact, and able to ship goods all over the world, the US was granted the unique power of printing the world's reserve currency. After all, if the devastated countries were going to buy American goods, they would need dollars to do so.

The winners throughout the world were sadly the central economic planners, popularized in America by economists John Maynard Keynes and Paul Samuelson. Government economic planning is considered by most university professors of economics to be superior to voluntary individual planning. Our college students have been taught for decades that it is possible to steer away from the extreme government planning of socialism, fascism, and communism to find a happy medium with Keynesian-type interventionism.

The flaw in this thinking is that the planners believe that individuals are incapable of doing the right thing for themselves. It is true that mistakes will always be made. But history has shown that a political/bureaucratic system planning for each one of us—even if it does so in a limited fashion—guarantees failure and corruption on a massive scale. Bureaucrats can never know what each of us should do with our lives and our money.

How can government satisfy so many demands and expectations when government itself produces nothing? This question is hardly ever asked.

Keynesianism is a philosophy that despises the libertarian principles of free markets, commodity money, no central banking, private property, voluntary contracts, and no deficit spending.

It is argued that some government intervention is needed to assure "fairness" to all. However, the Constitution does not give authority to Congress, the executive, or the judiciary to use force to "run the economy." Further, once force is introduced, the special interests take over. Economic interventionism always morphs into the worst form of cronyism that inevitably undermines the middle class.

Economic interventionism, which is part of the current system of government for most of the world, is supposed to achieve economic security for the masses without thugs running roughshod over the people and their liberties. The result, however, is an ever-shrinking middle class and worldwide anger at a super-wealthy class being rewarded by government favoritism. Instead of the people receiving economic security, crumbs are thrown from the plates of the elites to pacify the masses.

Controls are imposed by the authoritarians who have no respect for private property whatsoever. The property remains in the name of a supposed owner, but it is not his to decide what can be done with it.

Ownership becomes subject to the whims of bureaucrats.

In America, one does not really even own one's home, even after a mortgage has been paid off. Everyone who thinks he owns his own home is, in practice, merely a renter from the government. Property taxes act as the "rent." Try not to pay the taxes, and the government will evict you out of "your" home.

Property owned by average working people is routinely confiscated through eminent domain. When property is up for grabs in this way, the bribing of politicians and inspectors becomes the norm. The dealmakers conspire and benefit from this corrupt system at the expense of the poor and the less sophisticated.

Economic humanitarians are always claiming they have an answer for the needs of others at no cost. These do-gooders too often believe in their own nonsense.

When government seeks to control the economy and social behavior, the stage is set for big trouble. Under these conditions, economic and social rewards come from gaining influence in and control of the government.

Seeing regulations help some corporations at the expense of their competition prompts the poor, who suffer from bad policies, to band together to lobby for their share of the political pie. Aggressive power seekers fight over who controls the purse strings.

The bailouts of the 2008 economic collapse indicated who generally wins the contest—politically influential special interests, not the average person.

Realizing the financial straits in which we find ourselves today, many people are fearful and angry. They are vocal participants in exclaiming the horrors of our becoming a much poorer country.

The question is when will we accept the changes that are

absolutely necessary? When will people call for changes that will actually make a difference, instead of merely shuffling around the deck chairs? The mainstream media have not shown an interest in reporting the real crisis before us.

Government busybodies enjoy telling the people how to live their lives in order to be more virtuous in all their personal activities. This is done with the hope that people will be more creative and productive for the benefit of the state and society as a whole. This effort always fails since its goal is not achievable through government coercion. But the effort does destroy the concept of individualism, increase the power of the state, increase poverty, and lead to conflict between the factions who fight for their "entitlement."

An interventionist state needs a financier, and that is where the Federal Reserve comes in. Taxation alone is not enough to fund a leviathan state. The ability to create new money out of thin air acts as the beating heart of big government.

Originally, some restraints were placed on the ability of the Federal Reserve to print money at will, but, after President Richard Nixon closed the gold window on August 15, 1971, the dream of getting something for nothing became official world policy, benefiting the United States the most.

When Nixon closed the gold window, he removed the last restraint on the Federal Reserve's ability to create new money out of thin air. Before Nixon's action, dollars were merely receipts for gold, though Americans could not exchange the dollars for gold. Decades earlier, Americans could trade in their paper dollars for actual gold ounces. But FDR abolished that in 1933.

Until the gold window closed, foreign governments and central banks had retained the ability to trade in their paper dollars for gold. After the massive money printing by the Fed to finance the Korean and Vietnam Wars abroad, as well as President Lyndon B. Johnson's "Great Society" welfare programs at home, foreign governments and central banks were trading in their dollars for gold at an accelerating rate.

It is at that point that Nixon and the US basically defaulted. Nixon "closed the window." Instead of letting foreign governments and central banks rightfully trade in their dollars for gold, they would get stuck with the paper.

Closing the gold window resulted in everyone being stuck with paper dollars. No one in the world could trade US dollars in for gold. This enabled the Fed to print these dollars with reckless abandon, which it most certainly has done ever since 1971.

So the question must be asked: Who benefits? Why the marriage of government and banking? We know from history that a marriage of church and state produced horrific consequences. Are we just supposed to accept the marriage of banking and the state as a fact of life?

What's in it for the government? Well, direct taxation, that is government directly confiscating your earnings at the point of an IRS gun, can only go so far. Eventually the people revolt when direct taxation gets too high. But, if the Federal Reserve is granted a monopoly to print as much money as it wishes, that alleviates the government having to directly tax the people more. The people still pay their direct taxes, but now government can tax them even more without the people knowing it.

Now the government can create brand new Treasury bonds and the Federal Reserve can buy them with money created out of thin air! The government can finance whatever it desires—warfare, welfare, anything!

The Federal Reserve is the financier of big government. If you have a problem with big government, then you have to have a problem with the Fed, since it is the great enabler. And, as always is the case, government expansion must come at the expense of personal liberty.

Politicians, because of the Fed's printing press, can make promises without worries of where the money is going to come from. The Fed is always there to finance it. This Fed-supported spending helps to secure reelection for politicians as support comes from those who directly benefit from the new money. It turns out to be a convenient partnership between the spenders in Congress and the Federal Reserve.

Media and university economists jumped on board at the very beginning. They began preaching and teaching the fallacious belief that debt and the creation of credit by a central bank is equivalent to wealth, which is pure fiction. Even to this day, many believe that this system is here to stay.

Endless welfare for the poor (and the rich) would be the new nirvana. Gold as money, which acts as a restraint on reckless government expansion, was accordingly tossed away. Governments hate gold because it cannot be created on a whim. You cannot print more gold. This very fact acts as a restraint on big government.

But now, with money that can be created with a few keystrokes on a computer keyboard, the stage is set for the destruction of mankind by allowing it to be buried in a bonfire of paper money and credit.

The end of this system is fast approaching. The financial and political elites may close their eyes to this reality, but the people are starting to wake up to the fact that there is no such thing as a free lunch. The end is near for those living on "free" stuff. The special interests, from the military-industrial complex to crony Wall Street firms to the medical and media companies closely connected to the government, will be greatly affected. Major adjustments are necessary.

The Keynesian system can no longer afford the militarism overseas and endless entitlements at home. The results and tone of the recent presidential campaign reflected the anger that the average American feels. Without a significant correction in our thinking about this economic system, the problems and the anger will grow a lot worse.

We saw a few previews as to what lies ahead when the financial markets were ravaged in both 2000 and 2008. Since 2008, we have muddled through a period of economic sluggishness and lack of true prosperity. We have experienced a form of pseudo-prosperity, financed by exponential borrowing and creation of fiat dollars.

This cannot continue indefinitely, and the longer the occurrence of the necessary correction is delayed, the worse the next crisis will be. Tinkering with a failed Keynesian model will be no more successful than would any tinkering by Mikhail Gorbachev with the collapsing of communism in the Soviet Union in the late 1980s. There was no saving communism, and there will be no saving the Keynesian paper empire.

Government economic planning eliminates the "invisible hand." Market-determined prices are far superior to the distortions created by price-fixing central planners. Market prices give us an indication of the supply and demand of resources, labor, and every other market factor. Entrepreneurs and businesses need accurate prices in order to make rational and sound decisions.

When government interferes in economic activity, prices become distorted. Supply and demand are not accurately relayed to entrepreneurs. As a result, individuals and companies are led to make bad decisions. They may take out loans because the Fed has artificially suppressed interest rates, when, if interest rates were set by the market, they would not have taken out the loans.

The Federal Reserve creates illusory booms. People experience what is known as the "wealth effect." In other words, real wealth has not been created, but the infusion of new money creates the illusion that it has. The financial crises of 2000 and 2008 were the illusions being shattered.

In fact, it is an error to call the illusions being shattered a "crisis." Instead, this development is actually a return to economic reality. Adjustments have to be made with downsizing and the elimination of debt that should never have been taken on. The real crisis is the Federal Reserve creating the illusions in the first place!

The Federal Reserve's booms cannot last forever, as each "crisis" that we go through painfully reminds us. Supply and demand cannot be repealed. Economic law must always win.

The artificial boom and bust cycle created by central banks is not reserved for the US alone. All over the world, and throughout history, this cycle has played out with a predictable regularity.

Oftentimes, extreme authoritarians capitalize on the financial busts. They ride the anger of the populace into political power. For example, Germany's bust in the 1920s is closely related to the rise of Adolf Hitler.

There were many other examples in places like China, France, and countries in South and Central America. In Zimbabwe and Venezuela, we have recently seen economic crises involving hyperinflation. Not only must the populations suffer economically when the busts take place, but tyrants are often waiting in the wings to dispense political pain as well.

Today the entire world stands vulnerable to a similar situation since essentially all major governments have endorsed massive money printing in an attempt to restore economic growth. A giant, unparalleled Ponzi economy has been created worldwide. Never before has there been a situation where fiat currency has dominated world financial markets for so long. And there is no historic evidence that fiat money can endure when contrasted with the thousands of years in which the gold standard existed.

There is always a limit to the amount of debt that a nation can manage. The crisis comes when paying the interest on the debt becomes overwhelming. The huge correction that is coming will soon challenge the political stability of the world.

The notion that printing more money and accumulating more debt will solve our problems is a pipe dream. Eventually, the people will demand their money from the banks or real value for their dollar purchases. That will be met with policies similar to what have been recently implemented in India that prohibit cash holdings and gold purchases, prompting the economy to seize up. When the unwinding starts in a serious manner, it will create chaos, fear, and political upheaval like we have never experienced before.

Despite the writing being on the wall, establishment economists remain convinced that "capital" and low interest rates should be a function of smart people running the central banks of the world. Instead of recognizing that capital is the result of savings and production, they insist that capital can be created by just printing money. They are convinced that there is neither a need for a commodity currency nor for market rates of interest controlled by savings.

One should not expect a warning from establishment economists or the mainstream media. They will be caught flatfooted as always. The usual responses of "no one saw this coming" and "no one warned us" will be common.

The anger expressed by the victims is frequently justified but poorly understood. If people are unaware of what is causing rising prices, why the value of their money is falling, and why standards of living keep dropping, how are they supposed to rationally come up with a solution?

It is natural for people to look for someone to blame, but that someone never happens to be the actual cause: The Federal Reserve. The central bank always seems to skate by when the finger pointing takes place.

The media do their part to keep the status quo intact as well. In a very predictable manner, the media start to blame "free markets" or "corporations" or "greedy businessmen." More government and, often, more power to the Fed are the go-to solutions!

Denial by both the media and mainstream economists is to be expected. It is not easy to accept the notion that the system is technically insolvent and philosophically bankrupt. Cognitive dissonance sets in, and the addiction to easy money and the "wealth effect" become difficult to overcome.

Politicians likewise do not want to give up political power, and those on government assistance do not want to stop receiving unearned benefits.

Partisan bickering over which presidents are responsible for the good times and the bad times is merely a sideshow. Presidents, with their influence on tax and regulatory policy, can influence how long a recession lasts after it begins. The more government intervention, the longer the recession. But, the truth is the cycles of the ups and downs are a consequence of Federal Reserve monetary policy.

Presidents do, however, take credit for the Fed's illusory booms. They attempt to capitalize politically by claiming it is they who are responsible for the "good times."

This political ploy just helps to confuse people as to who really runs our out-of-control government. The people are purposely distracted by elections that never end up resulting in a change in course. When conditions deteriorate, some believe that all that is needed is different leadership and tinkering on the edges by those who claim they know how to favorably and fairly redistribute wealth by government force. The expectation that this will result in prosperity is a recurring illusion.

As hard as it may be for those who benefit from the current system, the acknowledgment of a flawed philosophy is a must. Ideas truly have consequences and a bad idea must be replaced with one that is good.

Libertarian economic thinking is the only real answer for dealing with such a mess. It provides the economic and political answers needed to rebuild the world financial system and to restore prosperity. It will be necessary for the leaders of the country to define exactly what the proper role of government should be in a free society, but that will only happen when enough people demand such action.

The Founders tried to give us a constitutional republic. But, the US government has drifted far from the course the Founders presented. All advancement of civilization has been dependent on improving the understanding and acceptance of the principles of natural rights and individual liberty. The time will come when we will have the opportunity to continue that process of advancing civilization.

4 Militarism and Empire

The Federal Reserve does not act as the US government's piggy bank for domestic interventions alone. The Fed is also the financier of America's military empire abroad.

Shortly before the Fed's founding in 1913, America had already had a taste of empire and its own colonies as a result of the Spanish-American War of 1898. Prior to that war, the US had a strong tradition of staying out of the affairs of foreign nations.

George Washington said in his farewell address: "'Tis our true policy to steer clear of permanent alliances with any portion of the foreign world."

Thomas Jefferson in his inaugural address listed "peace, commerce, and honest friendship with all nations, entangling alliances with none" among the "essential principles of our government" that would guide his actions.

Change came at the beginning of the "Progressive Era." Theodore Roosevelt, a progressive who is still lionized to this day, wrote in his 1917 book *The Foes of Our Own Household* that "we should regard with contempt and loathing the Americans ... crying on behalf of peace, peace, when there ought not be peace."

The new Progressive Era was ushered in by the US taking over Cuba, Puerto Rico, Guam, Hawaii, and the Philippines. President William McKinley even stated the following in an 1898 executive order regarding the imposing of a US military government in the Philippines after the US had signed a peace agreement with Spain: "we come, not as invaders or conquerors, but as friends, to protect the natives in their homes, in their employments, and in their personal religious rights ... the mission of the United States is one of benevolent assimilation."

Sound familiar?

Even to this day, the American Empire promotes itself as a "liberator."

It would only be a few years after the Spanish-American War, and after the new overseas empire was taking form, that a central bank would be needed to keep the war machine rolling. In 1913, the Federal Reserve was hatched.

The very same year, the income tax constitutional amendment was passed in America as well. This led to every American's income being presumed to be the federal government's property. The government then decides what percentage each American is allowed to keep.

Prior to the income tax, the only contact that the average American had with the US government was with the Post Office.

Richard E. Byrd, speaker of the Virginia House of Delegates, accurately proclaimed what was about to descend on the land of the free: "A hand from Washington will be stretched out and placed upon every man's business ... Heavy fines imposed by distant and unfamiliar tribunals will constantly menace the tax payer. An army of Federal officials, spies and detectives will descend upon the state."

The government was very slick in selling the income tax. At first, it only applied to the highest income two percent of Americans. This was just the laying of the net. Once the US—just four years later—made the fateful decision to enter World War I, income tax rates jumped many-fold. The income tax net has been yanked up so that many more Americans are forced to pay the tax. Most Americans seem permanently caught in the net.

Had the Federal Reserve not been created in 1913, it would have been inconceivable for the US to enter into World War I. How would it have been paid for? Taxation? Americans were bitterly opposed to entering a conflict in Europe that had nothing to do with them. In fact, Woodrow Wilson was reelected with the slogan "He kept us out of war."

Ludwig von Mises did not mince words when he wrote in his book *Nation, State and Economy*, "One can say without exaggeration that inflation is an indispensable intellectual means of militarism." "Without it," Mises continued, "the repercussions of war on welfare would become obvious much more quickly and penetratingly; war weariness would set in much earlier." The Federal Reserve is the great counterfeiter. It can inflate the currency to pay any bill.

John Quincy Adams declared, in his remarkable speech delivered to the House of Representatives on July 4, 1821 when he was Secretary of State, that America "goes not abroad in search of monsters to destroy." Adams explained the moral and practical reasons for adopting a foreign policy, which would today be labeled as "non-interventionism," reflecting a sound constitutional position. Adams's argument was that, even if the motives for getting involved in the affairs of other nations were above reproach and based on humanitarian instincts, with the intervention "fundamental maxims" of American policy "would insensibly change from liberty to force." If America followed that path, he said, "She might become the dictatress of the world." Adams presciently added that America then "would be no longer the ruler of her own spirit."

By 1917, with overseas colonies, the Federal Reserve, the Income Tax, and now World War I, the wheels of the American Empire were in motion.

The United States has been in almost constant war ever since, with a few years break between some major conflicts. But even during breaks, the CIA was performing its "regime change" operations covertly.

In essence, the "Progressive Era" has been an era of continuing war that carries on to this very day. Those who advocate for peace, non-interventionism, and the foreign policy that existed for the first 111 years of this country's existence, are considered of a bygone age.

The military-industrial complex always has a never-ending series of monsters that we need to destroy. There is always a new Hitler ready to be displayed on every magazine cover as the next target. Even though there is no threat of anyone invading America in an effort to take it over, Americans are kept in a perpetual state of fear.

In the early 1950s as fear was being promoted in the early days of the Cold War, Senator Ralph Flanders of Vermont said: "Fear is felt and spread by the Department of Defense in the Pentagon. In part, the spreading of it is purposeful. Faced with what seem to be enormous armed forces aimed against us, we can scarcely expect the Department of Defense to do other than keep the people in a state of fear so that they will be prepared without limit to furnish men and munitions."

Fear works. Decade after decade, the military-industrial-complex simply recycles the same tactics to keep fear and war alive.

From 1945 to 1989 the "monster" that served the purpose of providing profits for the military-industrial complex was Soviet communism. The real costs of the militarism pursued to oppose the Soviet Union were huge and include the deaths and injuries of fighters and the so-called "collateral damage" with the death of innocents in covert actions around the world and wars in Korea and Vietnam.

Today, the "monster" is "radical Islam." Both Republicans and Democrats agree that radical Islam must be eradicated by military force anyplace in the world that it might be found. President Trump brags about how tough and thorough he is in this effort, using it to justify massive increases in spending for the weapons of war.

The reason that there is some danger to Americans from radical Islam is because the real cause of the threat is denied. "Blowback deniers" will not consider the clear evidence that our aggressive policies in the Middle East since 1991 have provided an incentive for people to seek revenge for our occupations and involvement in just about every Muslim country in the Middle East.

The US presence is pervasive throughout the world. It has been reported by Zero Hedge that US Special Forces were deployed in 70 percent of the world's countries in 2016.

In every war, the mainstream media plays their part. War propagandists are dominant in the media that are not bashful about publishing "fake news." When couched in terms of exaggerated fear and excessive patriotism, along with exaggerated praise for our military, the demand to fight the "monsters" becomes overwhelming. Jingoism is a powerful tool for propagandists.

The war propagandists are very talented. American citizens roll over and end up supporting, even if only passively, the spending of huge sums of money that will supposedly keep them safe.

The real irony of this policy is that it consistently makes things worse. More jihadists are generated by the US invading countries overseas.

The errors are compounded even further when we ally ourselves with the very people we call the enemy. It is not infrequent that factions of al-Qaeda and other radical groups receive weapons from the US or join the US in fighting a supposedly common enemy, like has happened in the effort to depose Syria President Bashar al-Assad.

It is also not uncommon for the US to support brutal dictators, like Saddam Hussein in Iraq, only to depose them later. American support for hand-picked dictators enrages the people who, when they've had enough, strike back at us as happened in Iran in 1979 after the CIA had deposed Mohammad Mosaddegh and installed the brutal Shah who then ruled with an iron fist for 26 years.

The biggest lie comes from playing the patriotism card. Any objection to this failed policy elicits ridicule and charges that one is un-American and unpatriotic.

Endlessly we see the adulation for anything military. The military is placed on a high pedestal with constant praise for military members' service. This helps divert attention from the real costs in life and limb for the deeply flawed policy. It is all done with a straight face even though all the wars fought since 1945 have been unconstitutional and undeclared.

These wars have not secured even one iota of liberty for us. As a matter of fact, the opposite is true. The greatest threat to our Constitution and our freedoms has been our own government. We now live in a surveillance state with the Bill of Rights torn to shreds.

There is nothing to suggest that the new Trump administration will reverse this trend. The recent election and the heated debates did not address the issue of liberty or signal abandonment of the idea that we must continue to fight the monsters abroad. The fears continue and are always exaggerated. Our policies of interventionism are not being reconsidered.

Government interventionism, unfortunately, is alive and well in all areas of our lives. The federal government is not about to shrink. Without a big reduction in the US government intervention, we can expect just more of the same, or worse.

Trump is dedicated to continuing vast US military interventions around the world. Further, there is the prospect that, during his presidency, those interventions may expand significantly and new ones may begin, maybe, for example, against Iran or North Korea, regarding which Trump has spoken threateningly.

Trump has appointed recently retired and current generals to key positions. These include Secretary of Defense James Mattis who retired from the Marine Corps in 2013 and Secretary of Homeland Security John F. Kelly who retired from the Marine Corps in 2016. National Security Advisor H.R. McMaster remains an Army general. McMaster replaced Trump's initial appointee Michael T. Flynn in the position. Flynn had retired from the Army as a general in 2014. Gen. Kelly has since gone on from Homeland Security to become President Trump's Chief of Staff.

I am concerned that the combination of Trump's apparent openness to escalating, expanding, or starting anew military conflicts along with his surrounding himself with high-level advisors—both generals and neoconservatives—who see military action as the go-to option means that there will be significantly more war during his administration. We are already seeing this develop, with actions including Trump ordering attacks in Syria on the Syrian military, deploying more US troops to Syria, announcing a record-dollar-value arms deal for Saudi Arabia that the US is aiding in its attack on Yemen, expanding the use of drones for targeted killings around the world, and talking tough about Iran and North Korea.

Where would the US government find the troops to support a major expansion of US military intervention? One possibility is reinstating conscription. Though the military draft was ended decades ago, young men are still required to sign up with Selective Service. Women may soon be required to register with Selective Service as well. In 2016, the requirement that women register for the draft seemed closer to a reality than ever before. President Obama expressed his support for the idea, and the Senate even included such a requirement in its version of the National Defense Authorization Act, only to have the requirement removed when the bill was considered in a House and Senate conference committee. With women now allowed to serve in military combat roles, some people are arguing that the next step in ensuring fairness and equality is to require women to sign up, like men, for inclusion in a future draft.

The draft certainly was not applied to Trump when he was a draftable age. During the Vietnam War, Trump received five draft deferments.

The US foreign policy of the 21st century has significantly contributed to the massive migrations coming from a war-torn Middle East. And these migrations have contributed to the serious political disruptions now ongoing both in Europe and in the United States. The social-political upheavals of the never-ending war machine has brought the unbelievable migration of millions of people to other countries and cultures. The chaos is extraordinary.

The citizens who are subjected to the unnatural, politically-inspired immigration, take the migrants in and must also pick up the tab. If anyone objects, the race card is automatically played and the critics are charged with xenophobia and hate.

Voluntary integration has existed with differences in race, color, and creed with success many times throughout history. But, the use of force to mold people and decide cultural and economic conditions is not playing well and will not be accepted by the people who are victimized by the New World Order. As a matter of fact, the exact opposite will be the result, with greater racial and cultural conflict in the future.

A libertarian approach, using the principles of natural rights, private property, and voluntary exchanges in all associations, solves the problem. Working toward peaceful prosperity for all concerned can never be achieved by permitting government aggression for molding society. If that approach is used, it will always be at the sacrifice of liberty, peace, and prosperity.

Lies are used to start and continue the wars. Most of our wars, even the aforementioned Spanish-American War of 1898, have relied on lies to mobilize the support of the American people.

Many jingoistic arguments were used when the warmongers hyped up propaganda to unnecessarily get the US into

World War I, which turned out to be neither in any way related to our national security nor "a war to end all wars." Instead, is turned out more to be the war to "start" all the wars of the 20th century that would follow.

Support for World War II, which was basically a continuation of World War I, was built by President Franklin D. Roosevelt's twisting of the information the American people received.

Since the turn of the 21st century, it has been commonplace to have the war propagandists, made up of the media, the military-industrial complex, and neoconservatives, lie us into constant multiple wars in the Middle East. None of the wars during the past few decades had anything to do with national security, the Constitution, or defending freedom. They have been driven by the special interest groups that control our foreign policy.

The discovery that our government and media consistently deliver "fake news" has caused reasonable skepticism of all news sources. This is a very encouraging sign, but the enemies of truth are eager to use government censors, working in combination with social media companies, to censor all news in the name of protecting free speech. Their goal is to silence the truth-tellers so that lies are all that the people hear.

All governments tend to lie "for the people's good." The larger the government and the more power it has, especially in an empire or military dictatorship, the greater is the need for more lies in order to maintain power. Truth then becomes treasonous in an empire of lies.

Seeking out only ethical and moral people to be placed in government does not solve the problem. It never works. Big government is the problem. It is a system that eventually breeds lies, corruption, and offensive wars, causing a steady erosion of personal liberty.

The supposed "humanitarian" foreign policy of the US government over the last 25 years, especially in the Middle East, is an ongoing tragedy of gigantic proportions. Just as "patriotism is the last refuge of a scoundrel," "humanitarianism" is the first excuse of the self-righteous.

The US government has no authority to become someone else's boss. Good intentions are self-deceiving and a tool to satisfy the desire for self-importance.

All sides suffer in humanitarian intervention. Americans, who end up paying the bill for the government's generosity, become its victims. Americans also end up having to sacrifice their liberty.

Meanwhile, the recipients of humanitarian efforts are rarely helped in the long run. Inefficiency and excessive costs eventually bring these programs to a halt. Humanitarian programs involving foreign aid very rarely help the people in need, as the funds are frequently stolen, wasted, or used by enemies in a civil war.

The claim that our ideas would favorably remake the Middle East was a sick joke. Sending young Americans to die or be maimed, killing hundreds of thousands of Muslims thousands of miles from home, and spending trillions of dollars on unconstitutional offensive intervention is beyond the pale.

On top of this, when Americans see wounded veterans not receiving proper care, it only adds to the disgust they feel for our government. That rage has been expressed over the last several years. Since the problem remains and keeps getting worse, some real answers are needed.

Our intentions are always said to be "exceptional" as we

force Third World nations to hold elections as we do in this country. Of course, we never tell those that we occupy about the corruption that occurs in our elective process. The Third World countries that are the recipients of our "exceptionalism" are provided funds for the transition to a political system that we endorse. True success is very rare in this effort.

Whether government tries to run our lives at home, or attempts to "remake" people in other countries across the world, the inevitable result is misery. This process has given a severe and shocking blow to Western civilization, which was built on the opposite principles.

It has been said that, in this world of ours, "all good will be attacked." Whether it be weeds that attack the garden, or tyrants who attack our liberty, the principle is the same. All good must stand up to that which will inevitably attack it.

In addition to dangers from economic central planning and from the military empire, Western culture has been under relentless attack from the ideas of "Cultural Marxism." These ideas have been gaining momentum and have been creating mental prisons for individuals. These insidious ideas are the next topic for us to consider.

5 Cultural Marxism, Self-Reliance, and Morality

Karl Marx's predicted united workers of the world tearing down existing governmental systems in order to create a Marxist utopia did not occur. Nothing could compare to the unbelievable amounts of wealth that capitalist nations were producing. So Marxists were shut down from an economic angle.

This would not stop them, as a re-branding of Marxism would take place. Western culture would become the next target. If Marxists could not win from an economic standpoint, they would instead launch an attack from a cultural standpoint. A form of cultural terrorism would be unleashed in Western countries, including America.

Cultural Marxism is ruthless. Not only does it engender an entitlement mentality and a never-ending stream of fictional new "rights," it also tears apart the moral fabric of a nation.

Cultural Marxists believe that, if you strip away the values of the people in Western nations, new values could replace them, values that are consistent with the ideology of Marxism. Americans may have had the largest middle class in the history of the world, but their intellectual establishment would jump on board with Cultural Marxists with much enthusiasm.

Divide-and-conquer would be the strategy. The idea of individuality would have to be replaced by seeing people as parts of groups. Those groups would then be used, targeted, and victimized. Groups would be pitted against one another based on sexuality, skin color, age. A war of all against all.

From this we would get the ideas of "multiculturalism," "political correctness," "social justice," "diversity," "tolerance," "sustainability," and "environmentalism." As the notorious "community organizer" Saul Alinsky wrote in his book *Rules for Radicals*, "the organizer's first job is to create the issues or problems."

If Western nations were not willing to get on board with Marxism economically, the Marxists would strike back and attempt to tear Western culture apart piece by piece.

American universities have been a breeding ground for Cultural Marxist ideas, which are essentially mental prisons that define what a person can say, what he cannot say, what he can think. The concept of universities helping students expand their knowledge and exposing them to new, challenging ideas has been turned upside down and inside out. Rules regulating multiculturalism and free expression are overbearing and are destructive to a learning environment. The incessant hours of debate over who should use which bathroom is much higher on some universities' agendas than teaching math and science. Responsibility for this failure should be placed squarely on administrators and boards of directors of the universities.

The decline of the American educational system is a major factor in the anger directed toward our government. This is because of the system's promotion of ideas that are now playing havoc with America's society. Huge costs, lousy education, a lack of real work training, and student debt burdens that are unpayable are additional negative results.

American high school students now rank roughly 31st among students in developed nations in math achievement. The notion that the use of vouchers will reverse this disastrous trend is overly simplistic. Only a lot more homeschooling and private schooling, competing with the government education monopoly, can help.

The education situation is so bad that it is hard to believe that the failure is not achieved deliberately by those who thrive on chaos and who are planning to remake our society. The leaders of government education are anxious to head off any inroads of the libertarian message that offers the real solution.

There is nothing to indicate that our universities and government school system have any intention of challenging the collectivism of the 20th century, nor the threat that Cultural Marxism poses in the 21st century.

The principle of nonviolent discrimination, which means employing free choices in all our social activities, has been completely rejected. Picking and choosing our friends and associates is permitted, but not whom we hire or what we pay our employees. Those decisions are now limited by politicians and bureaucrats because the protection of private property has been grossly undermined.

In a free society, everything from the use of bathrooms to wages is decided by voluntarism and individual rights. The system that we operate under today is authoritarianism and results in various groups allying with each other to bully other groups. Liberty is never the objective. There is never any recognition of the fact that voluntary associations, which exclude aggression, are far superior and can help achieve the cultural cohesiveness that most people desire.

"Social justice warriors" should be referred to as social warriors AGAINST justice, property, and liberty.

It is an obsession of social justice warriors to strongly endorse the use of government force in order to set social rules. Nothing less will suffice. That is their modus operandi. A New World Order is their goal, and they recognize that religious beliefs and spirituality must lose their influence because these are also seen as a powerful enemy to a monolithic secular world government.

Many people are sick and tired of factions in our society playing the race card for political gain. Saying "black lives matter" while trying to silence other people from saying other lives matter too is nothing more than a tool to cause racial friction by claiming victim status due to racial bias. This of course frequently incites racial hatred.

A very popular tactic of Cultural Marxists is the artificial creation of "rights." The tactic evidences a fundamental misunderstanding of exactly what genuine rights are. The fictional view of rights usually does not include the most important ingredients, which are the natural rights to life, liberty, and the ability to keep the fruits of one's labor. Instead, social justice warriors seek authoritarian control of the economy and forced redistribution of wealth for the sake of "fairness" or "equality." They see the government as being responsible for providing food, jobs, and anything else that is demanded.

Because the social justice warriors reject or trivialize natural rights and property ownership, their efforts will ultimately diminish prosperity and end up hurting the people they say they want to help.

Natural rights come in a natural way. They are granted by the Creator, as the Declaration of Independence states. Natural rights precede the government. They are not a gift granted by the government.

We must always remember that anything a government can give, it can just as easily take away. In addition, anything a government can give, it must first use force to take away from someone else, thus violating that individual's natural rights to his own property.

America's educational and political systems have conditioned most citizens to see rights as bestowed by government onto special groups. This is a part of the Cultural Marxism playbook to divide and conquer, as well as to institutionalize victimhood status.

But rights do not belong to groups. They belong to individuals. We should never refer to certain groups as having a "right" to secure special privileges. We should not refer to corporate rights, gay rights, women's rights, minority rights, handicap rights, indigent rights, homeless rights, illegal immigrant rights, or any other designation of rights by religious, ethnic, or other group affiliation.

Lumping people together into groups to compensate for injustices only sets the stage for endless turmoil between different groups. It leads to an "entitlement mentality."

This entitlement mentality is not something that just the indigent believe in. It is an attitude that is pervasive throughout all income brackets. The wealthy are well aware of how governments provide benefits to big corporations like the weapons manufacturers and the financial conglomerates, as well as plenty of other corporations, organizations, and people who are represented by effective lobbyists.

Governments can, through regulations, tax code provisions, abatements, eminent domain, artificially low interest rates, and many other means, provide special benefits to satisfy the political demands of the wealthy elite for "their" entitlement.

Meanwhile, in the inner cities, where poverty and violence are a consequence of government policy failures, the "entitlement mentality" helps produce anger when more government actions do not improve conditions.

Government should never act beyond its authority to protect liberty. When government places controls on peaceful activities, whether cultural or social, and takes on the role of policeman of the world, respect for actual rights (i.e., natural rights) is diminished.

As long as entitlements are seen as "rights," the authoritarian state will grow. Such a system will always reduce productivity and wealth while requiring ever greater use of force to secure the goods and services for those who believe they are entitled to them. When the people realize that the system is no longer functioning, they inevitably rebel.

The end of the interventionist economic era is near. The solution cannot be found in expanding government force. Indeed, it is the immoral use of government aggression that has undermined the market system that was once the engine of production and the source of middle-class prosperity.

The role of government in a free society must be limited to providing an environment where the release of creative energy and ignition of the desire of self-reliance can thrive.

Some people claim that they deserve "reparations" for previous injustices that they or their distant relatives, were subjected to in the past. The big problem with this is the people who must do the compensating are guilty of nothing. They are not responsible in any way for the past injustices.

The reparations process violates the natural rights of those forced to pay.

Applying natural rights principles, it would be immoral for the government to order such reparations given that the reparations would require stealing from the innocent to compensate for the misfortune of another. Compassion is one thing; forcing welfare transfers by calling them entitlements is quite another.

The entitlement mentality did not originate in the Constitution. It has been advanced in America over the past 100 years by progressives who could not have cared less for the principle of liberty in a constitutional republic. Acting in accord with the entitlement mentality has not only harmed liberty and helped free the US from constitutional constraints; it has also helped bring America to a precarious financial position. The fact is that eventually all welfare-warfare states self-destruct since they are very costly, are frequently paid for by debt, and are extremely inefficient. They have never worked throughout history.

Also, there is no self-satisfaction from being dependent on others, no matter how tempting it might be to enjoy the benefits from other people's work and effort. Self-reliance, achieved through assuming responsibility for one's own life in all ways, produces a much greater abundance of self-worth—a virtuous goal that is not available to the victims or beneficiaries of an authoritarian state.

Recently I had a wonderful experience that demonstrated ideas relating to entitlements, self-reliance, victimization, and how one should handle excessive government-sanctioned aggression.

West Columbia is a small town 20 miles from my home in Lake Jackson, Texas. A historical marker was unveiled by the Texas Historical Commission in April of 2016 honoring a special citizen in the town who had died in 1920.

Not many people knew much about the fascinating life of Charlie Brown before the unveiling ceremony that came about due to the efforts of a few people. Brown was born a slave in 1828 in the part of Virginia that is now West Virginia. John Quincy Adams was the president at that time. Details of Brown's life as a slave are sketchy.

At the beginning of the Civil War in 1861, Brown's owner moved to Brazoria County in Texas—the county in which I live. After having lived as a slave for nearly 40 years, Brown gained his freedom after the Civil War ended.

Brown could not read or write, but he had a remarkably successful life after gaining recognition of what was rightfully his: the natural right to his life, his liberty, and the fruits of his labor. His story revealed that he never looked back, and that he did not belabor his being a tragic victim of a legal system that denied respect for his rights from the time of his birth.

How Brown was able to achieve so much during the rest of his life is a remarkable story. Brown died at the age of 92 in 1920 as a millionaire (in 1920 dollars). This was the same year that Warren Harding was elected president.

Zelda Talbert, a granddaughter of Brown who lives in West Columbia, said she did not remember her grandfather but recalls her family saying that he bought land for 25 cents per acre.

Brown's great-grandson Clark Woodson is 69 years old and lives on some of the 3,000 acres accumulated by his great-grandfather. When I interviewed Woodson on the Ron Paul Liberty Report, he told some fascinating tales of this unique ex-slave's life. Woodson said that, though his great-grandfather could not read or write, Brown could "cipher." Brown knew his numbers. And Brown obviously had a superb business sense and a superior work ethic. How else could an individual, after coming out of circumstances of life as a slave for nearly 40 years, eventually own 3,000 acres, or, as reported in the Houston Chronicle, about two-thirds of the city of West Columbia?

Brown purchased a plantation with a large two-story house on it, where his wife Isabella once worked as a slave. Brown and his wife moved in as the owners of that house. What an irony! At his death in 1920 Brown was the wealthiest black person in all of Texas. He accumulated and ran several productive businesses, which included a gristmill, sugar mill, sawmill, syrup mill, and cotton gin. His employees were white, black, and Hispanic, as were his customers.

It was said that Brown was one of the first people in the area to own a radio and a car, as well as to live in a mansion. The two-story mansion he chose to live in was purchased from across town and he had it moved to his favorite spot in downtown West Columbia. This in itself was a significant feat.

One of Brown's first purchases was Brazos River land, which was thought not to be worth much since it was "cluttered" with cedar trees. With ingenuity and foresight, Brown cut down the trees (without a government permit) and sent the lumber down the Brazos River, with much of it going to northeastern coast furniture makers as far away as New York. Successes like this encouraged him to keep buying, keep working, keep hiring, and keep making money for new purchases. His first purchase of land was thought to have been in 1869.

Charlie Brown was a generous philanthropist. He donated land for schools and churches, usually for use by former slaves and their families. Even today, a school building stands on land Brown donated to the community. A street in downtown West Columbia continues to bear his name.

This story has a powerful message for today's society, especially considering that what Charlie Brown accomplished was rare, even for the average person who never endured decades as a slave, while remaining illiterate throughout his life. Business judgment, willingness to take a risk, hard work, and refusing "victimization" were valuable traits that Brown cultivated.

It is difficult for our current society to accept the notion that no one has a "right" to free food, shelter, clothing, a job, medical care, or education. Needs are not rights.

The main goal in a free society is to strive for equal justice under the law. The freer the society, the greater will be the incentive for people to pursue ambitious self-reliance while rejecting on moral grounds the use of aggression to get what they want.

Charlie Brown responded to acquiring his liberty in a positive and productive manner by depending on his own merit and ambitions. After escaping from the monstrous condition of human slavery—the complete opposite of the condition sought in libertarianism—he pursued a productive life and achieved unbelievable success under dire circumstances. Brown did so in spite of the fact that most other former slaves never achieved similar results after emancipation.

Brown achieved his business success without a Small Business Administration loan, or any government grants or subsidies. Best of all, Brown was not confronted with government laws and regulations that would have added a great burden to his efforts to pursue his goals. He did not have to deal with OSHA, the EPA, the Fish and Wildlife Service, property controls, sales taxes, income taxes, or competition from competitors that were subsidized by the government. Not being confronted by numerous government laws and regulations was critical to Brown's ability to assume responsibility for himself.

Brown's many employees voluntarily accepted the wages that they and Brown agreed to. With acreage costing between 25 and 50 cents per acre, Brown's employees probably received pennies per day in wages. Both sides, workers and the owner, were pleased to work together to achieve a successful business. This allowed for the creation of many jobs that provided people with the means to purchase goods and services. It also produced wealth for Brown that, as a consequence of Brown's philanthropic attitude, was used to benefit the community.

Brown's life and legacy obviously turned out to be much more successful than if he had waited for a federal government program to help him after he was freed from slavery. As the Civil War was ending, all that Brown asked for was that which was naturally his: Liberty.

Liberty was key to Brown's success. As a consequence, liberty was also beneficial to hundreds, if not thousands, of other people. An interesting point that Brown's great-grandson made to me was that it was believed that Brown's customers and employees were mostly white. This is an example of how free markets can miraculously eliminate the sentiments of racism that are so prevalent today. I believe that racism today is directly related to the entitlement mentality and a misunderstanding of the significance of personal liberty and property ownership.

Charlie Brown reminds me of another former slave who, after emancipation, proved that looking forward, rather than backwards, allows one to achieve great things.

Booker T. Washington, like Brown, was born a slave and had an amazingly successful life in spite of all the disadvantages from which he suffered. Born on April 5, 1856, Washington, at a much younger age than did Brown, received his freedom from the bondage of slavery. Washington was nine years old; Brown was 37. Both, however had to be highly motivated to overcome the social and economic obstacles they faced and make something of their lives. Both set great examples for those who have been disadvantaged by circumstances beyond their control.

Neither man dwelled on his victimization. Instead, they both took actions that proved that personal liberty, in a free society, can provide the foundation for a life of productivity and self-reliance, along with personal satisfaction from one's accomplishments. Both Brown and Washington worked hard and struggled for success, and they did it on their own without depending on a government program. Liberty was the key.

Booker T. Washington's great success was as an intellectual leader, providing education for other former slaves and their children. His goal was to motivate them to become productive members of society. In addition to emphasizing economic liberty and hard work, Washington also argued and worked for ensuring full civil liberties for all people, something that he was convinced, in time, would come.

One of Washington's amazing achievements, that was his pride and joy and for which he was well recognized in his lifetime, was his starting and promoting the Tuskegee Institute, a well-known black college. Washington died at the young age of 59, while still heading up the Tuskegee Institute.

Both Washington and Brown endorsed nonviolence in promoting the cause of civil liberties, just as Dr. Martin Luther King Jr. did.

Interestingly, Booker T. Washington severely criticized black leaders who worked hard to promote the victimization movement. Washington claimed that they were not interested in developing self-respect and self-reliance. Being economically productive was of no interest to them. After emancipation, their goal was to continue the agitation and racial conflicts in order to blame the system and white people for all black people's problems.

Washington, in his 1911 book *My Larger Education*, astutely described the nature of some people's advocacy regarding black people. It is rather amazing how accurately Washington, over 100 hundred years ago, recognized what the vultures were up to. A quote from this book follows: "There is another class of coloured people who make a business of keeping the troubles, the wrongs, and the hardships of the Negro race before the public. Having learned that they are able to make a living out of their troubles, they have grown into the settled habit of advertising their wrongs—partly because they want sympathy and partly because it pays. Some of these people do not want the Negro to lose his grievances, because they do not want to lose their jobs."

Today, racial conflict is getting worse, especially with the political correctness obsessions that are now common. The entitlement system that has prevailed and that has caused so much harm to minorities and the middle class results from the constant emphasis on victimization.

Washington had early detractors, similar to some voices we hear today, who claimed he was not doing a favor for former slaves by preaching about a work ethic, productivity, and assuming responsibility for oneself. W.E.B. Du Bois, a very strong critic of Washington, was demanding full civil liberties and rights and, at the same time, keeping "race" as the primary issue.

Du Bois, born in 1868 after the emancipation, was a dedicated supporter of communism. Du Bois rightfully defended total civil liberties for all blacks, which was Washington's goal as well. Their argument was over strategy and timing. But, just as do some of today's so-called black leaders, Du Bois detested the principles of free markets, property ownership, and self-reliance.

Many black leaders today, who declare their total allegiance to minority rights, in truth are the real racists seeking to make minority individuals dependent on government entitlements. It is all done in the name of economic equality (which is an illusion) and to promote communism and radical socialism.

The greatest threat to the early black leaders, as well as to the current black leaders, who advocate for government entitlements came from the examples of people like Charlie Brown and Booker T. Washington. Successful blacks who follow the lead of these two individuals by defending liberty and refusing to live at the expense of others are written off as being "no longer black."

The only chance for society to sort out this age-old dilemma will come with the understanding of the nonaggression principle of libertarianism.

America's Founders were well aware that a constitutional republic is fragile because it must compete with sinister forces driven by immorality, avarice, and mendacity. Throughout history there have always been individuals who sought power and used it to satisfy their own insatiable greed for unearned riches. They have a willingness to lie with impunity and suffer no reservations of guilt. The Founders' concerns were legitimate. The shortcomings of an immoral society cannot be solved through a more authoritarian government producing more laws, no matter how well intended. Only a free society can permit the goals of excellence and virtue to thrive.

Moral breakdown always leads to economic problems with a lowering of the standard of living for all people. Current events indicate we are close to some very major social and economic changes.

John Quincy Adams famously said: "Our Constitution was made only for a moral and religious People. It is wholly inadequate to the government of any other."

"[F]or avoiding the extremes of despotism or anarchy," Gouverneur Morris wrote, "the only ground of hope must be on the morality of the people."

Benjamin Franklin opined that "only a virtuous people are capable of freedom." Franklin continued, "As nations become corrupt and vicious, they have more need of masters."

Many other quotes supporting this point of view were put forth by other Founders.

Founders also quite frequently invoked religion as a strong guide for the people in incorporating morality as a necessity for securing liberty.

During the 20th century, atheistic dictators like Joseph Stalin and Pol Pot carried out slaughters that numbered in the millions. Some argue that the absence of religious beliefs was not the motivating factor of these killings. Even if that is the case, neither did religion restrain their actions. It is much closer to the truth that these vicious murderers of the 20th century, along with others including Mao Zedong and Adolph Hitler, came to believe that they themselves were gods. In modern times, one can look at North Korea's Kim Jong-Un as an example of this concept.

Over the past 50 years, the family as an institution has changed dramatically. Single-parent homes are commonplace. Abortions are now casually considered "birth control," rather than something done very rarely to save a mother's life.

Homelessness in America is epidemic but frequently hidden from sight. Each night, over half a million people are homeless, with many sleeping in shelters or outdoors. In New York City alone, it has been estimated that around 61,000 people, including 24,000 children, sleep in shelters. The magnitude of this problem and the complexity of the causes pose a great danger to society, especially if the next economic downturn is even more severe than the one from 2007 (which for many never ended).

In New York City, an interesting statistic shows that the Asian-American ethnic group makes up less than one percent of the homeless, under a tenth of Asians' representation in the city's population. Economic factors are important, but strong family ties, based on morality strongly adhered to in certain ethic groups, are crucial to making a free society workable.

Such social problems cannot be corrected by government mandates and affirmative action programs. A government that assumes responsibility for promoting excellence and virtue will produce the exact opposite. But, individuals understanding the importance of self-reliance in a free society can achieve excellence and virtue. When politicians and bureaucrats take charge, the people's liberties are destroyed along with the nation's wealth. The chaos that results demands an alternative, not just in management, but in philosophy.

The morality of a society is a reflection of the people and the standards they set for themselves as individuals and for their governing institutions. During the 1960s, especially in America, moral standards were changing rapidly. The deadly foolishness of the Vietnam War incited resentment and violence in our cities. In a short period of time we witnessed the assassinations of John F. Kennedy, Robert F. Kennedy, and Martin Luther King Jr. Sadly, our own government appears not to have clean hands in these assassinations. Evidence continues to mount connecting the CIA with the killings of the Kennedys and the FBI and local police with the killing of King.

The sentiments regarding life, liberty, and property have radically deteriorated since the 1960s. One of the most significant changes that occurred was cheapening the value placed on preborn life from what had existed since the days of Hippocrates, 400 years before Christ.

The Hippocratic Oath is approximately 2,400 years old. This is a pledge that physicians took to uphold ethical standards in ancient Greece. It was not a law written by the Greek government. It is an oath that new physicians have taken throughout the centuries—even up to this day, to some degree.

The thrust of the oath expresses the recognition, even in the early days of the oath, that a physician must "reject harm and mischief." Patient privacy and confidentiality was an important part of the oath. Sharing one's medical knowledge was an obligation. Refusing to administer a poison to anybody was a statement against euthanasia. Ethical and moral behavior with patients was clearly understood to mean that a physician should not take advantage of patients in any way. One of the best-known parts of the Hippocratic Oath, as originally written, was, "similarly, I will not give to a woman a pessary to cause an abortion."

Over the centuries, there were translation differences in and minor modifications to the oath. In the 1960s the changes became more extreme. The arguments made for the changes—some claim weakening—was that the Hippocratic Oath was overly rigid for a modern society that is different and more advanced. The argument went that the oath needed to be adapted to the spirit and sentiments of the times. During the 1960s and somewhat the 1970s, it became very unpopular to even bother taking the Hippocratic Oath because of fear someone might be offended.

I graduated from Duke medical school in 1961. I finished medical school six months early. By the time graduation arrived in June, I was off doing my residency at the Henry Ford Hospital in Detroit. So I did not attend the official graduation. I understand my class did not take any version of the Hippocratic Oath. The oath was either ignored or a changed version was used in the 1960s at many medical schools.

My son Rand graduated from Duke in 1988. Rand's class did recite a Hippocratic Oath, but in a watered-down version. Rand, with other class members, attended a voluntary baccalaureate service-type event held in the chapel the day before graduation.

The original oath essentially said "I will not do an abortion." One modern oath says "I … will give no drug, perform no operation for a criminal purpose, even if solicited, far less suggest it." This new language meant ethical approval for participation by physicians in the process of euthanasia, the death penalty, abortion, or military experimentation or torture, as long as the law permitted it. The law, i.e., the government, sets the ethical standards. Believe me, a lot of members of Congress that I knew did not qualify for setting ethical standards for anyone. The Hippocratic Oath had essentially lost its significance.

Some will argue, I'm sure, with my contention that these changes represent a society in which people have become less moral and less responsible for their actions. Granted, the Hippocratic Oath never created a society that entirely rejected abortion, but the oath had been used as a major ethical standard for more than 2000 years for most physicians. Then, self-imposed ethical restraints were replaced by guidelines issued by the state. While it may be claimed that we are now following government's ethical standards, it is a stretch to call it a continuation of moral standards that serve to improve society.

Over the last few years about one million abortions have been performed in the United States per year. The attitude regarding abortion changed significantly during the 1960s. Many abortions that were being done then were technically illegal. The national law was set by the Supreme Court in 1973 with the ruling in Roe v. Wade. It passed with a seven to two vote, using the "privacy" issue as the deciding factor.

Privacy was recognized for the mother—not for the unborn. The ruling declared that the live human fetus was not an entity that had rights. This is arbitrary, since the live human fetus does have inheritance rights, as well as a right not to be injured or killed in an accident or homicide, or by the malpractice of an attending physician.

The decision in 1973, as a direct consequence of a change in the morality of a nation that made acceptable what had been unacceptable a decade earlier, was an opening salvo for our society to subtly, if not explicitly, have less legal respect for life itself.

Defending liberty against the demagogues and authoritarians of all stripes is never an easy task. It becomes much more difficult when human life can be discarded in a bucket and society remains blinded to the moral significance of such an action. I see this dilemma as a moral crisis. If one cannot defend all life, how can the defense of all civil liberties be carried out? You have to convince yourself that what exists for nine months is no more than a blob of tissue that has no value and deserves no protection except for some special and arbitrary circumstances that deal with intent of injury or death.

And this is why it is not unheard of for a distraught teenager to deliver and dispose of an infant. One moment before birth it is considered a blob, not qualified for protection, and one minute after birth, when not much has actually changed, there is an outcry when the young mother kills the newborn.

The new mother who does this, though she may believe she is acting consistent with the moral standards of society in which she lives, can be arrested and found guilty of murder. A moral society would strive to resolve this contradiction. The significant changes in our moral standards in modern times need to be considered. The rebuilding of a failed society must incorporate the moral concerns for all life. More laws passed by a larger federal government are not the answer.

The rejection of traditional and ancient ethical standards is noteworthy. Ethics training for current MD licensing by the state include the proper way of filling out insurance forms. Confidentiality and privacy of patient health records have essentially disappeared in the age of government medicine. Courts have easy access to medical records. All insurance companies, drug producers, medical providers, and many government agencies are connected electronically, with almost all doctors being forced to comply. In 1996, Congress passed a law the Health Insurance Portability and Accountability Act (HIPAA) that is said to guarantee privacy, yet it guarantees easy access to all the health providers' records. The biggest intruder on medical privacy is the US government.

Today MDs participate in government torture. Though rare, MDs are involved to advise on just how far the torturers can go with the process without causing death. Medical experimentation by MDs in Nazi Germany and other authoritarian societies is well known and well documented by our own CIA. Our military has participated in such acts as well.

If the original Hippocratic Oath were applied today, medical doctors would not participate in carrying out the death penalty either. Instead, all decisions would be directed toward preserving life and not participating in causing death.

These changes in ethical attitudes are not mere coincidences. They represent a moral climate that disqualifies a society from successfully engaging in a constitutional republic. This type of society invites in a dictator to maintain order and to act as a terrible substitute for markets.

Basic morality is important in economic policy, social issues, and foreign policy. When self-reliance is discarded by both those who want to use power to dominate others and those who yield to the temptation of allowing demagogues to provide a so-called "free lunch," conditions deteriorate as they have in today's America. Authoritarians rush in with promises of economic security as a "right" and set the stage for sacrificing liberty for empty promises. The door for competing special interests swings wide open, and a continuous battle rages to see who can get in front of the line to grab the stolen benefits.

Without a moral basis for the promises made, we can only expect variations in the use of force by government to gain the greatest support for assuming control. Safety, security, and economic benefits are hotly debated, but it is difficult for the people to understand that we need a lot more than a management change. No one wants to admit and confront the significance of the end of a major era and its relationship to the moral standards of the people.

The great danger we face today is not just the immorality of the people, it is the immorality of government officials as well. The eventual result will be an end to our Constitution. History has shown that government always ends badly when people lack the virtue to defend liberty.

The major decline in the morality of our society is reflected in how whistleblowers are treated. Instead of being praised for revealing the truth about our government, they suffer the consequences of being put in prison or living with the threat of incarceration hanging over them. Some examples are Edward Snowden, Jeffrey Sterling, Stephen Jin-Woo Kim, John Kiriakou, Shamai Leibowitz, and Chelsea Manning. The threat of punishment also hangs over Julian Assange of WikiLeaks because his organization has published information provided by whistleblowers.

In today's society, the most serious crime an individual can commit is perjury—lying to the government. Perjury is seen as a serious attack on the power structure that controls the empire. Yet, the people know that the government routinely lies to them. There are times when lying to the government should be seen as acceptable. This is especially true with dictatorships. Lying to the KGB, the Gestapo, or any other similar corrupt police agency to save one's life should hardly be considered an immoral act. The big question is this: Are we approaching as dire a situation with policing actions in America?

The great strides made since the Magna Carta toward the king or government no longer being above the law have disintegrated.

The use of the IRS to go after conservative and libertarian groups has been well documented. And the illegal, immoral, unconstitutional killings carried out in secret by the CIA and hired assassins are never punished.

Our foreign involvement in dozens of countries has prompted targeted killings as part of the stated goal of "protecting our national security." President Barack Obama acknowledged that in fact "kill lists" do exist and have been used to justify even the assassination of American citizens without charges or trial.

If there is ever a public outcry, a commission is created to find out who is responsible and what went wrong. But I have learned over the years that, instead of seeking truth, commissions like the Warren Commission that investigated the assassination of John F. Kennedy or the commission that was supposed to find out the truth about the Iraq War inevitably cover up the mistakes made by or wrongdoing of our leaders.

When the current system implodes, the rebuilding will depend on what the intellectual leaders and the politicians with the greatest influence offer as a replacement.

The choice is clear. The choice is liberty or tyranny. There is no happy in-between. This choice should not be difficult.

6 Science Is Never Settled

The military-industrial complex is not the only group that understands the political value of generating fear. The value is also understood by those who work to create a relentless stream of hysteria in the name of "global warming" or "climate change." In fact, there are oftentimes articles in the mainstream media arguing why climate change is a bigger threat than terrorism. Then someone will try to rebut such an article by saying that, no, it is terrorism that is the number one threat.

Unfortunately for liberty, "none of the above" is never an option. Instead, Americans are expected to pick their poison. Do they want tyrannical government in the name of fighting terrorism or do they want it in the name of fighting climate change?

The propaganda that we must sacrifice our liberties to government so that government can better control the climate has crept into the media, crony corporate America, and (of course) government schools. In fact, there is a movement to introduce "climate literacy" into curricula of government schools, which is just more proof that government-controlled schools are used to indoctrinate kids on whichever political ideas happen to be in fashion at the moment.

The propaganda runs from ridiculous to hysterical. Mainstream media has published pieces claiming that free birth control is needed for women in order to battle climate change. There have also been arguments made in the mainstream media that climate change pushes women to become prostitutes.

This desperation seen in the media is largely the result of the fact that Americans have thus far shunned the propaganda and see the propaganda for what it really is: a tool for the transfer of unimaginable power to the federal government and international bureaucracies so that they may further micromanage our lives.

Further, Americans know very well that government lies … a lot. It lies us into war and creates one problem after another with its interventions. We are now supposed to believe that this institution should be tasked with fixing the climate?

One of the most egregious arguments put forth by the climate change brigade is that the science is settled on the subject. This is a very dangerous belief to latch on to.

After all, the idea that the Earth was the center of the universe was a belief commonly held by intellectuals up until approximately the mid-16th century when Nicolaus Copernicus said it was not so. It was "settled" from the beginning of time until Copernicus's challenged the theological and scientific "proof" that all heavenly bodies moved in a manner that placed the earth in the center.

Pseudoscientific thought prevailed up to just less than 500 years ago. Until that time, the scientific arguments promoted a passionate belief that was completely wrong. They looked outward and wanted to see the reality of the universe, but they had another agenda related to religious beliefs that led them to lie to themselves about science.

Even after the publication of Copernicus's On the Revolutions of Heavenly Spheres, the same year Copernicus died, it took many years for his assessment that the sun did not move around the earth but instead the earth orbited the sun to be accepted as basically correct. This indicates that, prior to Copernicus, science had not settled it. And even Copernicus's assessment of the universe needed many modifications.

The truth is that science often is not settled. It frequently only raises more questions.

Even Albert Einstein's theories of relatively did not settle science. To this day scientists continue to test and challenge Einstein's ideas. But no one better dare to challenge the opinion of the fanatics who preach the false doctrine of global warming and a prediction of the end of the Earth as we know it. There is no room here to debate the pros and cons of the current environmental convictions that are claimed to have been firmly "settled" by some scientists despite the fact that not too many years ago scientists were warning us of a coming new ice age.

My point is that anybody who claims "the science has settled it" on any issue that they have emotionally politicized should be challenged. Why does this type of issue need to be settled by partisan politicians and a majority vote, rather than by honestly pursuing scientific inquiry?

I am not making an argument for one side or the other on this issue. Instead, I am making a plea for not stifling inquiry into scientific questions. It is interesting to question why something is the way it is. That some people despise open minds continuing the study of scientific issues is very unsettling.

The only thing that should be settled in science is that

challenging conventional wisdom should always be permissible and that preventing people from doing so is neither scientific nor consistent with respecting free thought in a society that is supposed to be protecting the freedom of speech.

Those who dare question the climate change claims are branded as "deniers." The propagandists try to ostracize those who may not believe. Paul Krugman, in the New York Times, even attempted to portray denial as a sin! He wrote: "You can deny global warming (and may you be punished in the afterlife for doing so—this kind of denial for petty personal or political reasons is an almost inconceivable sin.)" It is now a "sin" to use your own mind to come to your own conclusions?

Just think, if scientific inquiry was shut down, not only would we not have the curious minds of a Copernicus, Galileo Galilei, or Isaac Newton, we would also go on believing that sunspots do not exist. Can one imagine the consternation of the global warming fanatics if science someday supports a theory that human activity AND natural events play a role in climate change? What then would the sunspot deniers do?

There need to be more questions, not less. There needs to be more debate, and not a rabid attempt to shut debate down. A few other areas I would like to see the conventional wisdom challenged regard the use of DDT, the overuse of immunizations, and US government involvement in dietary advice.

The mission of the enemies of a principled libertarian approach is to destroy the individual as an entity and make the masses subservient to the self-anointed privileged elite. Progressives believe they are all-wise evangelists, with perfect wisdom and understanding of what the proper humanitarian attitude for maintaining social order should be.

The dedication of the radical environmental movement smacks of a religious devotion. They may despise the conventional definition of religious beliefs, but at the same time they accept this fanatical devotion to environmentalism, as if it were their god.

7 The Deep State, Police State, and Surveillance State

The deep state, or "shadow government," is made up of banking elites, educational elites, major media, the military-industrial complex, and other establishment blocs. The deep state is the chief coordinator of government, no matter who the president happens to be.

Strongly influenced by the CIA, FBI, and other "national security" departments, the deep state seeks to control events with force, threats, and even murder if it thinks that it is needed.

Of course, copious amounts of propaganda are needed to allow the shadow government to operate as it does. A compliant media has always been advantageous for increasing government power. But now there is even a partnership of government with technology and communications companies. This too is vital for keeping any real change from occurring in the government.

Real change is not likely to occur until the system collapses. Voting the bad guys out will not succeed in overcoming the power of the deep state without an ideological "Revolution."

People are conditioned to believe there is actually a real

debate going on between the various candidates, despite the fact that, no matter who happens to be elected, the same policies are carried forward—more welfare and more warfare. Presidents tend to produce both, in ever increasing amounts, at the expense of Americans' liberty.

The real government, however, is not seen by the voters in our democratic elections. Murderous evil dictatorships of other countries are known, but our actual government is hidden from view. The deep state may be invisible, but it is ever-present and powerful. It has control over our financial system, foreign policy, and justice system.

Wars serve the interests of the deep state. The CIA has exerted tremendous power since it was created after World War II. Harry Truman, the president who signed the law creating the CIA, later lamented what the CIA had become. He wrote that he intended the CIA only to collect together and present to the president raw intelligence already available from various sources so the president could better assess the intelligence. He wrote that he never intended that the CIA "would be injected into peacetime cloak and dagger operations." This is from an editorial Truman wrote not too long after the assassination of John F. Kennedy.

The CIA is the political and military organization that carries out covert operations worldwide. It interferes in elections, uses torture, and overthrows or assassinates "disobedient" dictators who were supposedly once loyal to the US

Due to some excellent reporting and books written on the subject, more Americans are becoming aware of the inordinate amount of power that the CIA wields. Breakaway CIA rogue operations are carried out that even the CIA directors are not totally aware of or simply choose not to know anything about.

Mounting evidence indicates that the CIA was involved in the assassinations of both John F. Kennedy and Robert F. Kennedy. Acknowledgment and proof of a significant number of CIA assassinations around the world since World War II is now accepted by many.

In spite of Donald Trump's early harsh criticism of the CIA, my assessment is that Trump will relish the power he gains with control of the CIA and that he will use that power in a more personal fashion than have some previous presidents. He has been explicit in stating that "the enemy" should never know of his intentions. That of course will require the American people not knowing what his intentions are, and yet they are the ones who have to pay the bills.

This attitude will specifically apply to the global war on terrorism. No one, obviously, would want our enemies to know of our military plans in a constitutional, defensive war, but under most conditions since World War II it has been the American people who have been denied the information that they legitimately deserve when it comes imperialism overseas.

Secret CIA wars should be taken off the table (as well as preemptive nuclear strikes). In economics, there is a comparison of what is seen and what is not seen, as explained by Henry Hazlitt in his classic book *Economics in One Lesson*. A similar comparison can be made concerning the nature of "democratic" government. There is the government that is seen and used to pacify the masses. There is also the shadow government or deep state that is not seen and yet has the power to pull the strings of major economic and geopolitical events.

With the end of the current era of economic and foreign intervention approaching, the people have justifiably become suspicious of and have lost confidence in government. The big question is this: Is it really a rejection of both the government that is seen and that which is not seen? Since few people understand what the deep state is all about, that does not appear to be the case.

The foolish war on drugs, combined with strict regulations of private gun ownership and a deeply flawed judicial system, have created a huge time bomb in most of our large cities.

Even cities not suffering from excessive inner city violence are facing a funding problem with bankrupt pension systems that will surely expand the law enforcement problems.

Though domestic terrorist attacks are extremely rare, the federal government has been accelerating the militarization of our cities. With a former Marine Corps general now in charge of the Department of Homeland Security, no one should expect a smaller presence in local law enforcement. Ordinary American citizens will be bumping into a lot more federal law enforcement officials, including from the FBI, IRS, Fish and Wildlife, OSHA, EPA, TSA, FBI, FEMA, DEA, and ATF, throughout the country.

As always, it is argued that sacrificing a little liberty is a small price to pay for our security. But the questions that no one wants even to ask are: What if it is our own government that presents the greatest threat to our security and liberty, and isn't that what the people should fear the most?

The majority of Americans believe that the most important function of government is to provide safety and security, both economic and physical. The security that they seek includes the security provided by a military that would defend us if we were attacked by another nation.

As James Madison wrote, "No nation could preserve its freedom in the midst of continual warfare." Since the US government is involved in continuous warfare, our liberties here at home must come under attack as well.

Today, we are supposed to accept that the US military should be obligated to fight third-world countries that are 6,000 miles away and have not attacked America. This view is advanced by the Bush Doctrine that says the US is obligated to take the fight to them and initiate a war against them. The grave danger such fighting is said to counter is all too often based on lies.

The support for sacrificing liberty at the expense of safety blossomed after the 9/11 attack.

An effort to understand 9/11 as a consequence of our aggression in the Middle East requires that American politicians understand the nature of "blowback." If they did, they would never promote the lie that we are required to take our fight to countries in the Middle East and pretend that we go there to defend our country's liberty and the Constitution. What a lie!

Once a people accepts the notion that the purpose of government is perfect safety, liberty becomes a secondary issue, and it is assured that any beneficial results of such a policy are doomed.

More bureaucracy and pestering federal police will solve nothing. The various federal policing agencies are designed to curtail liberty and spy on the American people. They do not honestly deal with the failed global war on terrorism. They make it worse.

Attaining personal safety depends more on an individual understanding the Second Amendment and assuming responsibility for his own security than on government action.

Dependency on any federal or local police system is highly imperfect. Perfect safety would require a police guard at every home and every business. This obviously is not possible, and, if we even try that approach, it would be like protecting a herd of cattle by fencing the cattle in.

Seeking economic security through government is similar in a way to seeking physical safety through government. It is always couched in humanitarian goals of preventing anybody from falling through the cracks. The problem is that efforts like this have been tried numerous times throughout history and they always make the cracks bigger, allowing more people to fall through them!

The worst example is the total failure of the communist system, which caused millions to die and the state to obliterate any respect for liberty and justice. Fascism works in the same way: death, war, starvation, and no protection of liberty. The authoritarians' efforts in running government, even if starting with compassion and good intentions, always grant excessive power to the state and eventually destroy liberty while economic security is never achieved.

Only the politicians and bureaucrats in such a society seem to maintain economic security, and they do so through force and intimidation, and never by any productive effort. In the end, even the administrators of any command system are frequently impoverished as well.

The nature of the Vietnam War, with the lives lost, the hundreds of thousands of Americans wounded, and the victims of Agent Orange, contributed to a culture of drug use, which since then has grown to epidemic proportions. The use of drugs became commonplace and that attitude saturated our society here at home, especially among those of college age. The 1960s society reflected a distinct moral change in America's culture.

The ridiculous war on drugs, as a reaction, served only to exacerbate the problems of addiction, crime, and an unfair judicial system that was used against minorities. This only made race relations worse. These events and other changes that became prevalent in the 1960s have continued to play a role in the inner city violence that has become epidemic. The frictions have festered and have been made worse with today's entitlement attitude, the race baiting, and a militarized police force that is incapable of calming the violence of our cities. There is no indication that the Trump administration will act any more sensibly. Trump has promised to be more aggressive in the federal war on drugs, despite the many reasonable state challenges to abuses in law enforcement that we see today.

The 1960s saw philosophic and moral changes with regard to life itself. The Vietnam War made life cheap. Drug use made life cheap, as did the war on drugs. Inner city warfare made life cheap. The military draft made life cheap. Liberty was made cheap too. A sense of self-worth was also cheapened, and that fueled the fire of disrespect for the rights of others.

The SWAT team approach to apprehending suspects has gone awry. There have been too many examples of unarmed people being shot by overly aggressive police officers. This problem of course is compounded by those who turn police brutality and even poverty into strictly racial issues and encourage the hate-filled lawlessness that such characterizations can encourage. Unfortunately, there is little understanding as to why a bad economic system is a consequence of government policy. There are always people who claim that the bad economic conditions are a result of the failure of the free market, and they make their case for more authoritarian economic planning. This foolish cycle needs to be ended. My suggestion is simply this: Try liberty for a change.

Others have offered different answers that they claim, if followed, would provide an enlightened path to achieve safety. President Trump argues that the federal government has to make our inner cities safe again. At a Florida rally in February of 2017, Trump declared this: "Safety is a civil right, and we will fight to make America totally safe again."

The only problem with this is that "safety" in itself is not a civil right; liberty is. Trump's argument is that the government has not been aggressive enough in prosecuting criminals. However, the original intent of the Founders was that this would be an issue left for the states to deal with. To accomplish what Trump wants requires a strong government that seeks to protect us from ourselves. That effort is destined to fail. It cannot be done, and, if tried, liberty would be destroyed in the process.

A major tactic that government uses in the name of "safety" and "security" is the relentless invasion of our privacy. This tactic is perfectly backwards. It is the people who have the right to privacy and the government that must be transparent. Instead, we have an ultra-secretive government that spies on us constantly.

There is very little that the government is supposed to hide from the American people. The Constitution lists no authority for the government to operate in the dark, hidden from the taxpayers. But, the Constitution does explicitly establish strict rules barring the government from violating the privacy and safety of all citizens. The Fourth Amendment speaks to this issue in a clear fashion.

We now have a government that knows more about us

than we know about ourselves. The NSA, with the cooperation of technology and communications companies, can watch our every move. The government has access to every financial transaction, credit card purchase, and banking activity that we perform.

Freedom of speech is threatened by the super snoops who spy on everything we say on Facebook and our cell phones. We live in an age where our government constantly snoops and threatens us with censorship. The IRS knows everything about us financially and has even been used for political ends. Proponents of liberty, the gold standard, antiwar sentiments, and Austrian business cycles theories are all threatening to the Republican and Democratic establishment. They are frequently under surveillance and threatened with punishment for expressing these views.

The two agencies of government that are the most protective of their secrecy, but that also participate in destroying the people's privacy, are the CIA and the Federal Reserve. Neither one is subject to a legitimate and thorough audit.

The Pentagon, with its runaway spending habits, is one of the most wasteful government operations. Sometimes I wonder whether the members of Congress care at all about this. The Pentagon seems to get unlimited funds, and it is always asking for more, if for no other reason than to create jobs, even though the weapons it produces are frequently not needed and many do not even work.

But there is never a thorough audit of the process. In 2016, it was found that the military deliberately kept $125 billion of military administrative waste hidden from the people so spending cuts could be avoided. Russia spent $66 billion on its military in 2015. We waste twice that much in one year. Nevertheless, the axis of evil in the Senate (i.e.,

Senators John McCain, Lindsey Graham, and Tom Cotton) cannot wait to provoke a war with Russia because of the threat it supposedly poses to Americans. Common sense should tell us they do not know what they are talking about. Their stands are, however, in line with taking care of the military-industrial complex.

We are drifting towards a dystopian nightmare. Under attack from the deep state, the police state, and the surveillance state, liberty is on the rocks.

Fortunately, despite these very real and very dangerous threats, there is much to be optimistic about.

8 The "R[EVOL]ution" Ahead

Our government's use of arbitrary aggression against its own citizens, as well as against countries abroad, should not be tolerated any longer.

It is well understood that when individuals use aggressive force on others to get their way a serious crime is committed that justifies a penalty. Yet Americans, as well as people around the world, have foolishly granted government agents the ability to legally get away with taking such actions. In America, government consistently perverts the moral law that the US Constitution was supposed to define for a constitutional republic.

On the one hand, people are rightfully punished for lying, cheating, stealing, and killing, but, when government agents do the same thing, it is called "serving the people." It is rightfully illegal for an individual to steal. Yet, the government routinely steals by counterfeiting money and taxing the incomes of productive Americans. And the government cheats by granting favorable contracts and special regulatory benefits to friends who financed electoral victories. It has been this way for a long time, but it is time for change.

This double standard contributes to the anger and disgust

that people feel concerning the government and is a reason they demand that government be reined in. Yet, thanks to the operations of the deep state, government is never reined in.

Changing the political parties or politicians in charge does not make a difference. Barack Obama was supposed to end George W. Bush's wars. Bush promised a humble foreign policy. Bill Clinton declared that "the era of big government is over." Ronald Reagan said that "government is the problem." Obviously, since these are the ideas that get politicians elected, it works to make the promises. But in every case, the promise is broken. No one reins the government in, even a little bit. It should be no surprise that the American people are angry!

It is the idea of liberty whose time has come. The need is obvious; the moral basis underlying a free society has been advancing for thousands of years and is now more refined than ever before. The task is to explain and popularize the moral imperative of transitioning into an era that fully endorses the voluntarism of the many over the coercion of the few.

The new era is still up for grabs. The wealthy elites will try to create a new system that will be acceptable to the people who are precipitating the current revolt. If the right outcome is not achieved, human progress will flounder. If the outcome is to advance toward a libertarian system, the cause of peace and prosperity will benefit with a positive step forward.

We find ourselves at a crossroads, and the course we choose in an attempt to get us out of the mess in which we find ourselves is vital.

It is my opinion that, if it is peace, prosperity, and human dignity that we seek, we must correctly assess the past 100 years of American history. The "Progressive Era" has produced monumental disasters. Government cannot better society by using aggressive force.

We must decide what our moral obligations are to ourselves and to others. We must promote a government that is strictly limited to protecting the natural rights of all citizens.

Achieving a productive and peaceful society is not a complex issue. The foundation is straightforward. Releasing creative energy can be done with a government designed to protect liberty, rather than one that seeks to run our lives, run the economy, and run the world. Permitting all peaceful activities should be the goal.

"Peaceful" means the absence of all citizens and government entities using aggressive force. Government can no longer get a pass. If we cannot do it, neither can government. No more double standards.

There must be a willingness to tolerate activities by others that one may find personally offensive, but that harm no one. There should be no concessions that government is entitled to play a role in protecting us from ourselves. A simple rule to be followed is the rejection of use of violence to control others, whether Americans or a foreign entity. Following this rule would give the world its greatest chance for achieving peace and prosperity.

Achieving these goals will be a challenge. As America's Founders have warned, only a moral society can assume the responsibility for ensuring the conditions necessary for a free society to succeed. A desire for liberty on the part of the people and a government limited in authority to protecting liberty are required. The principle of equal justice under the law and protection against the violators of a nonaggression standard are also crucial.

There should be no prior restraint on voluntary and peaceful activity, on the assumption that something illegal or dangerous might be done. This principle should apply to all economic transactions and personal interactions.

The social and political consequences of a libertarian society would be greater prosperity and a more peaceful world. This is indeed a challenge to the conventional wisdom of today's politicians worldwide. A libertarian society does not come about simply by rearranging what government interference is being employed. Neither does it depend on just changing the management of central economic planning. And it does not rely on wiser social engineering. Instead, the authoritarian principle of government must be challenged by the REVOLUTION.

Libertarianism rejects all use of aggressive force to change things, even if the planners claim humanitarian goals and especially if they claim a moral responsibility to perform certain actions. Humanitarianism is too often used to convince the people to willingly give up their liberties for the false promises of tranquility, prosperity, and fairness.

Tolerance of others can be a real challenge. Tolerance of different religious beliefs that reject coercion is fairly well understood and accepted, but personal social habits are not as easily tolerated.

In a free society, people are actually allowed to be mean, nasty, rude, selfish, ignorant, and biased, as well as to practice political incorrectness. It is for the individual to decide if he will make moral and compassionate choices. Discriminating in choosing your friends and household guests is acceptable. Libertarians believe that this principle should apply to all private property. Access to property must be decided by the property owner who may exercise the right to pick and choose his associates, visitors, lovers, friends, or customers. Your life and property are yours to control.

Being self-centered or even selfish, or having crude or bad habits, is not something that government authorities have a right to punish or interfere with. Mean and nasty people, as long as they do not violate another person's rights, should not be banned or excluded by the government from participation in activities. Private businesses, however, should be able to exercise their right to exclude. Take the restaurant that banned Trump voters from being served. The business exercised property rights, and, in doing so, showed that idiotically motivated discrimination can result in boycotting that effectively answers a business's action without making a federal case of it. Bad manners should and can be dealt with by families, churches, and friends, through persuasion and by setting an example.

Libertarians are strong defenders of the First Amendment, since it was correctly intended to protect controversial speech, not just casual conversation. Protecting the right to criticize one's own government is high on the agenda for the defenders of freedom of speech. Today, government monitoring of every word used on the internet, including social media, has created a great danger to this cherished liberty.

Momentum in regard to surveillance is now against liberty, and, sadly, the more divisive our society becomes, the greater will be the political excuse for giving the authoritarians more surveillance power, further eroding our privacy and curtailing freedom of speech. It is claimed that this surveillance is done with "good intentions." Similar claims are made about government efforts to silence and punish surveillance whistleblowers. But, it is never good to protect the people against those who tell the truth about what the government is up to. Only libertarian thinking can stop this movement to surveille us, control free speech, and drift toward a dangerous tyranny.

Objections to liberty have been abundant ever since liberty was first recognized as being necessary for the advancement of civilization. Understandably, authoritarians always resist challenges to their power. For progress to be made in restraining tyrants, who have for millennia controlled the general population, understanding liberty is necessary. Tyrants can only maintain their power by using force and lies, while targeting individual liberty as their enemy.

Today, major arguments against liberty are that liberty is impractical and that those in charge need to take care of the people. Taking care of people's needs has always been the excuse, while the real reason for tyrants assuming authority is to wield power to secure their material gain by taxation, which is theft, rather than by earning the money themselves. This dilemma has been around since the beginning of time, but it does not need to continue unabated. A libertarian society can better deal with the problems that the interventionists claim only they can solve.

Economic concerns regarding wages, safety, the environment, trade policies, prices, and insurance do not require government intrusion either. For example, a libertarian society would not require governments to provide bank deposit, flood, or medical insurance. It is hard for some people to understand that the market can actually provide these services with greater efficiency and much less cost. Yet, rules that conform to the principles of private property and voluntary contracts are fairer and more successful than the alternative of a bureaucratic, political system that invites big money into the process.

Voluntarism is peaceful and rejects all government favoritism. Recognizing the importance of voluntary contracts is crucial. For a free society to be successful, contracts must be respected and honored. Laws against theft, fraud, and causing injury to another person or another person's property are acceptable in a libertarian society. Eminent domain laws, however, which serve powerful special interests or government, would not be permissible.

What is needed is an understanding of the right to own property, along with working hard and delivering goods and services in an honest fashion, just as Charlie Brown discovered once he gained his freedom and became so successful in employing these principles.

If no aggression is permissible, it means that we, as a nation, cannot engage in unconstitutional, unnecessary wars to advance the vague desire to protect our "national interests" anywhere in the world against governments that pose no military threat to America.

Libertarians reject all prior-restraint regulations on goods, services, and speech. However, that does not mean that there would be no regulations in a libertarian society. A market-driven economy actually creates stricter regulations for protecting the environment, for example, because property rights may be enforced against polluters. In the current system, big corporations, including banks and drug companies, have a lot of influence in writing the regulations that handicap their competitors who do not have the financial wherewithal to "buy" protection in the tax and regulatory codes. A libertarian society would shut off this government-provided advantage.

In a libertarian society, there are strict rules against fraud, cheating, stealing, and causing bodily harm. If both citizens and governments accepted these strict rules, one can imagine how wonderful the results would be. However, libertarians recognize that most people, while they accept these restraints on individuals, rarely understand that the government must be held to the same standards.

It is a fallacy, believed by many, that it is a libertarian society following the nonaggression principle that would be chaotic and lawless. The opposite is found to be true. Just look at our society today with the record number of prisoners we incarcerate, and the many laws and regulations we have on the books. We actually have a greater percentage of people in prison than the communist government in China! Generously writing rules has done nothing to nurture a law-abiding and peaceful society. The current system we have reflects the failure of a non-libertarian society. Drug laws, for instance, have not decreased the use of drugs, but have dramatically increased criminality and violence.

A few simple rules endorsed by community leaders can create far in excess of the so-called benefits of a strong "law and order" society. If one looks closely at the multitude of laws that control our lives and diminish our privacy, one finds that these laws are responsible for many violations of natural rights. These violations are more excessive than those committed by the criminals in the streets. The rules were intended to punish the violators and instead did the opposite. They made the government a powerful violator.

Healthy globalism, built on commodity money, free trade, and voluntary exchanges can replace the ugly kind of political globalism that exists today. International coercion from globalist governments always fails to produce prosperity. It creates the atmosphere that we are now witnessing with a growing support for populism, protectionist tariffs, and currency wars. The libertarian alternative can replace the populist alternative to the failed international order. A more peaceful and productive international order can only be achieved with a libertarian foreign policy.

The dictators of the 20th century and the economic theories of interventionism dominant in the past 100 years were driven by ideologies that supported the use of government aggression, both domestic and international. But, a new day for liberty will come. The philosophic groundwork for liberty has been growing ever since the Keynes-Samuelson interventionism was accepted by mainstream economists and the political elites. Support for liberty also came from the European remnant that opposed the failed fascist and communist systems during the 20th century. The failures of those systems motivated people to discover and be interested in libertarian ideas as an alternative. Good things are now available for all concerned, if the world chooses to advance civilization by acceptance of a libertarian philosophy.

Great strides have already been made in spreading the message of liberty even though the politicians in Washington and elsewhere are oblivious as to what is going on intellectually. The politicians are quite aware of the anger at and rejection of current government management and are eagerly searching for ways to politically capitalize on it. However, except for a couple dozen members in Congress, US representatives and senators are uninformed as to the real causes of the crisis and how the principles of liberty can provide the solutions.

There are now hundreds, if not thousands, of organizations and groups in America and throughout the world that are advocating free markets, private property ownership, and sound money. There is also a growing consensus that the Federal Reserve and central banking in general are not friends of average people seeking to improve their lives.

Many states are now acting on their own by practicing a form of nullification in the area of the drug war, as well is on the monetary issue, legalizing marijuana and insisting that gold and silver may be used as legal tender as the Constitution mandates.

Groups like the Mises Institute, Young Americans for Liberty, the Future of Freedom Foundation, Antiwar.com, Zero Hedge, and many private homeschooling programs all contribute to the spreading of this wonderful message of liberty and peace.

Very few people, when informed, will oppose a philosophy that provides the best chance for the maximum number of people to enjoy peace and prosperity.

The failure of government, which will continue to worsen, will encourage many people to move in the direction of promoting liberty—out of necessity. Essentially, natural instincts are for freedom. The culprits are government demagogues. But their credibility is being diminished on a daily basis, and that is good.

The real boost for the liberty movement will come when it is recognized that libertarians never start wars, nor do they condone the government's power to steal from the people while subjecting them to the constant abuse of aggressive authoritarians. Libertarians physically threaten no one. Intellectually, they threaten all authoritarians.

The noisy bickering that we constantly hear today from all around—from Republicans, Democrats, conservatives, liberals, and all the special interests—is petty and represents efforts by groups of politicians seeking to gain political control over each other. We are currently not witnessing a serious philosophic debate between liberty and tyranny. That debate, however, is what we need.

Foreign policy arguments are just as non-purposeful. By dwelling on the misleading patriotic cries for protecting "our national interests" and making us safe from the phantoms of evil attackers about to destroy our way of life, prominent arguments steer the American people away from a noninterventionist foreign policy. Searching for "monsters to destroy" is a full-time occupation for those who believe that constant war is inevitable, necessary, and helpful.

The incessant fearmongering and the pretense that preemptive war is required to defend our Constitution, our lives, and our liberties is a false claim. It is argued that we fight them over there in order to avoid fighting them over here. The sick irony is that it is this policy of imperialistic intervention overseas that leads to blowback attacks and government undermining our liberties here at home. This policy also fuels the financial crisis that we face today.

The real debate ought to be between free markets, sound money, and personal liberty on one side versus Keynesian economic interventionism, fiat money, unlimited deficits, and total disregard for the importance of liberty on the other side. The debate should also include neoconservatism, warmongering, imperialism, and preemptive war versus a policy that rejects all forms of aggression, personal and governmental.

Libertarians are adamant in their support of the political system that provides the best chance for achieving peace and prosperity for the maximum number of people. Authoritarians are equally adamant that the system they champion is the best political system.

Each side is confident that the system it promotes is the correct one. Some people then would argue that the contest is just between different forms of government management with each side arguing that its "Mr. Know-It-All" is superior to the other side's "Mr. Know-It-All." However, much more is at stake than just picking the best manager.

Libertarians are opposed to all forms of government that use aggression to have their way and that are not committed to protecting natural rights. Libertarians reject aggression and say that anything peaceful should be permitted. Authoritarians, in contrast, argue that only that for which government gives permission is allowed. This authoritarian form of government is dependent on the use of violence.

For authoritarians, a group that includes most people in Washington, DC, giving a tax cut to the people is called a "cost" to government that has to be "paid for." The proponents of this view believe that government owns us and all that we produce, and that we should be allowed to keep only the portion that government allows us to keep. This is not too far removed from the beliefs used to justify enslaving the serfs of another period in history under feudalism. Libertarians reject this concept of redistribution and consider it equivalent to theft.

Authoritarians argue that anything that is not prohibited by the Constitution is permissible. Libertarians instead argue that only the authority explicitly given to the government and written in the Constitution is allowed.

The authoritarian has things backwards. If there is to be any government at all, it should be solely for the purpose of protecting natural rights—something that comes to everyone in a natural way. We should not start with the premise that government can do whatever it wants unless explicitly prohibited by the Constitution.

The political contest should not be over which variety of authoritarians we should tolerate. That is hardly a choice. The contest has to be between libertarianism and authoritarianism or between freedom and slavery for a true REVOLUTION to occur. Otherwise, liberty doesn't have a chance.

Authoritarians also endorse the idea that the government needs to prevent individuals from making bad choices. Backing this transfer of power to government is the hope that government will never make bad choices for us. But, government is incapable of protecting people from themselves. The belief that government can keep us from making bad choices has done a lot to undermine the principles of liberty and has significantly contributed to the mess we are in today. Giving up any liberty to the government guarantees that the government's method of achieving a stable society will be through the use of force, not persuasion.

Libertarians have total confidence that a free society is far superior to any other system. This confidence is dependent on "negative" knowledge. Libertarians admit they do not know how to run other people's lives and that they have no authority to do so. Likewise, libertarians understand that the individuals who have earned some income should decide how it should be spent. Providing an environment based on liberty and nonaggression, which will encourage excellence, virtue, and creativity, is totally different from assuming government bureaucrats and politicians can replace the energy that freedom generates.

An important point to remember is that the money involved in politics is a symptom of excessive government power, given that the government effectively auctions off benefits that are paid for by robbing the people. The moral replacement for this warped system cannot be imposing more regulations and targeting waste and fraud for elimination. Waste and fraud, after all, are natural and guaranteed consequences of an authoritarian government.

A true REVOLUTION for liberty must rely on convincing the people that sovereign individuals, in a spirit of voluntarism, should tolerate how others live, whether socially, religiously, or economically, without having to find those choices to be to their own liking. As long as it is peaceful, it is permissible.

Libertarians consider the nation-state a threat to liberty. It implies the joining together the political, i.e., the state, and cultural entities of a nation. This joining is fraught with danger. The power held by the nation-state explains much of why Cultural Marxism has been able to play havoc with our society in an increasing fashion over the last couple of decades.

The nation-state involves a variation of the conditions that one finds in a theocracy. It only exists by the use of political force. It is not in line with the libertarian approach needed for the crisis we face. In fact, the nation-state moves in the opposite direction of the course I am suggesting, which is to totally reject using government force to alter a country's cultural and personal ethical standards. A nation-state breeds super-nationalism—a system incompatible with a libertarian society. In economics, that nationalism is called corporatism or fascism.

Skepticism about the human condition improving in the near future is justified. The 21st century inherited many problems that were generated by the 20th century infatuation with various forms of excessive government interference in the lives of Americans. Personal liberty is on the wane. Endless international conflicts are draining our resources. The debt bomb is about to implode, and few people in Washington understand its significance. Violence emanating from the culture war is rapidly escalating. Corruption in government is epidemic. Anger flourishes as a result of false expectations and the evil it generates.

But my optimism remains. There is no reason to accept the premise that solutions to these many problems are not available to us. I am convinced that a single rule, if the people would accept it, would lead to a tremendous reduction in the problems that we face.

We must not forget that huge changes can miraculously occur in a relatively short period of time. The development of the steam engine that ushered in the Industrial Revolution, for example, brought about seemingly magical improvements in the human condition. The industrial era was possible because of an enlightened understanding of liberty, property, and economics that welcomed the benefits of self-reliance and self-ownership.

Very few people realized beforehand that the material well-being of average people would benefit tremendously from the Industrial Revolution, but that is what happened. So too can mankind today improve the chances of achieving peace and prosperity with a simple rule relating to interpersonal relationships.

The simple but powerful rule is this: REJECT AGGRESSION. NO PERSON OR GOVERNMENT ENTITY SHALL EXERT AGGRESSION OR VIOLENCE AGAINST ANOTHER PERSON OR HIS PROPERTY. AND STICK TO YOUR PROMISES.

The skeptics are right regarding the short run. Not much will change in the immediate future. Acceptance will take quite a while as it did with the development of the under-standing of natural rights and free markets. That took several hundred years of development before the full extent of Industrial Revolution occurred. But we must remember that in context of the history of civilization this is a very short period.

This effort should not be ignored. Defining and promoting the rules of rejecting aggression is crucial. There is no reason to be locked in on the idea that human civilization cannot make progress. Actually, all we need are more people to follow the age-old admonitions that originated with the early recording of history that the people should avoid lying, cheating, stealing, and murder.

A great assistance for popularizing libertarian society would be for the people to practice voluntary compassion for the unfortunate. Americans are already super-compassionate. With an economic system that massively increased prosperity, this generosity would expand exponentially.

Because of the nature of man, we should not expect that a perfect world can be developed. The world is made up of both good and evil, and even the nonaggression principle will not act as a panacea for all of man's ills. But it must be set as a goal if civilization's progress is to continue.

A better world is a goal worth seeking, and it is achievable. Reaching the goal depends on people accepting the notion that aggressive powers be denied to all authorities in government. This removes the incentive for the "bad" people to seek a government position because there is no power to be gained from such positions. The evil people will be reduced to "street thugs," with a lot less power to do harm.

Just think—no more preemptive wars, no more government counterfeiting, no more government theft, no more undermining our natural right to control our own lives as we pursue our happiness on our own terms.

The ultimate guide: ANYTHING THAT'S PEACE-FUL!

9 Final Thoughts: What to Expect and What to Do When the Crisis Hits

This book basically looks at the long-term prospects for liberty's success, which I believe are very positive. In the short-term, I have maintained that the entire world faces major economic and political problems. The coming global crisis will be of great magnitude and will involve domestic violence, economic consequences, and international conflicts. Though I'm a long-term optimist, I sense that the turmoil coming is probably on our doorstep and will present great dangers to a significant majority of the world's population.

Over many years while in Congress I expressed concern over the coming of dangerous economic and foreign policy events. Many have materialized. I have, over the years, been cited for correctly warning of future events like financial bubbles bursting and useless wars being fought that would inundate millions in the Middle East as a consequence of our totally senseless foreign policy.

This does not represent clairvoyance on my part. It's more an interpretation that bad policies lead to bad results. Understanding the downside of certain policies and a little common sense regarding human nature permits one to anticipate logical consequences in the future. Precise timing of events, however, is not possible.

The long-term, for me, is looking at the world in blocks of time of possibly 100 years or so. For instance, the Progressive Era that started at the turn of the 20th century introduced economic and foreign policies to the United States that have led to predictable consequences from which we suffer today. The many problems that we now have should surprise no one.

We should look forward to real progress in the future for promoting liberty. But for now that concept, though intellectually understood, is not yet politically acceptable. Dealing with the short-term is the major challenge we face today. That involves burying progressivism and providing answers to the existing problems it has created this past century for us and for the world. The length of the "short-term" is totally arbitrary and mostly refers to the immediate conditions resulting from bad government policy. The long delays in "fixing" the short-term result from an unwillingness of special interests who benefit from the status quo to give up on the ideas of interventionism that caused the problem in the first place. This prolongs the problems by not getting the government out of the way and permitting the liquidation of debt, mal-investment, and excessive government manipulation of monetary, economic, and foreign policy. An unwillingness to decrease the total amount of government spending is almost universally resisted.

These corrections need to be dealt with before the benefits of liberty can be achieved. Ideas are key. Ideas have consequences. Good ideas need to replace bad ideas. I am frequently asked when this major crisis will hit, what will it look like, and what plans should be made to deal with it on a personal level.

When Will the Crisis Arrive?

One of the most common questions I get is: When will this overwhelming major event occur? Though common sense reveals likely consequences, the precise timing of the event, which many will agree is coming, is not predictable. My assumption is that the great contraction or required correction has already started. In spite of the many optimistic government reports, half of our population is unhappy, poor, resentful, and angry. When the full-blown crisis arrives, leaving no doubt in the minds of anyone as to its seriousness, it will be readily apparent before we see a new president take office.

The precipitating event that will cascade through the world financial markets and engulf massive geopolitical crises will arrive in the dark of night. Most will be surprised and will respond by demanding more government intervention, which was the actual origin of the problem to begin with. The bankruptcy of a large financial institution, a large corporation, or a country going broke may well be the event that sets off the alarms that leads to the final blow up.

A major military conflict is becoming more likely every day with the various military activities in the Middle East and the escalating domestic violence in Europe. This could lead to an old-fashioned war with troops battling for strategic territory almost any place in the world, or even some kind of out-of-control cyber war.

The economic and social foundation of the world is fragile and vulnerable. The economic system is more precarious than ever. A dollar crisis may erupt resulting in the dollar losing its status as the reserve currency of the world. This would be an event of great significance and would affect the entire world's financial markets. The greatest threat comes from the huge total world debt that is unpayable and must be liquidated to get sustained economic growth started once again. When a dollar crisis begins, more debt and monetary inflation will only lead to more chaos with a threat of tyranny taking over.

The fear of the short-term serves to postpone any effort for liberty to reassert itself for the long-term. But it must be dealt with. It's not going to go away by applying worn-out economic theories to appease those who demand unlimited entitlements.

The long-term conclusive end to the Progressive Era has been anticipated and should not surprise anyone when it happens. Friedrich Hayek talked about the end stages of government interventionism in his classic "Road to Serfdom" (Published in 1944). Sadly, but probably correctly, he expected that the central economic planning that gained acceptance in the 1930s would lead to a nation of serfs, run by tyrants.

It was John Maynard Keynes, promoter of so much economic mischief in the early part of the 20th Century, who Hayek condemned and warned about. Keynes, in my estimation, was the individual who essentially popularized the concept that short-term "benefits" were more valuable than long-term economic consequences. It was obviously an easier sell to promote benefits for one group of voters at the expense of another, especially if the beneficiaries who enjoyed the unearned benefits were not recognized by the victims.

Frederic Bastiat, in his famous book *The Law* (1848), talked about the economic principle of: "that which is seen and that which is not seen." Being able to deal with only the short-term is a politician's dream, because the immediate benefits from government spending are "seen" and appreciated while the payment and lost opportunities are "not seen." Though the wealth is illusionary, it invites more of the same policy for which the politicians get the credit. It's a great trick until the bills come due. That's now and what this crisis is all about.

Henry Hazlitt in his fabulous dissertation on economics, "Economics in One Lesson" (1946), developed the "parable of the broken window," introduced by Bastiat. He further developed these ideas in explaining that the "short-term," which was readily visible and thought to be a panacea, was instead a deception and a dangerous economic policy.

The temptation to endorse short-term benefits at the expense of future planning is a powerful driving force in economics. Keynes in his "A Track on Monetary Reform" (1923) wrote about the "long run." His famous statement to refute the economists who disagreed with him on policy and had expressed concern about future consequences has been repeated thousands of times. Keynes' opinion was simple and clear and implied that one need not worry about the future problems as a result of economic planning, since: "In the long-run we are all dead."

Some have argued that too much is written into this quote and that it did not mean that Keynes lacked concern for future economic conditions. But it is a fact that his policies and those of many economic interventionists that followed developed the system from which we suffer today.

His hostility toward gold — "In truth, the gold standard is already a barbarous relic" — ushered in an age of massive expansion of government, welfare, war, and the dangers of inequality of wealth distribution, which today is stirring class hatred and political chaos. These are the conditions that have put liberty on the ropes. Paying for the government excesses with "counterfeit" money may work in the short-run, but all counterfeit money, especially when issued by central banks, ends badly.

We now live in an age where instant gratification is a prime driving force for society. There's very little concern or understanding about how benefits are paid for, who pays for them, who produces them, or what future negative consequence will arise from concentrating on the short-run and dismissing the long-run. Numerous Keynesian-type economic policies aggravate the discrepancy between the short- and the long-term. They include things like: savings and thrift is not beneficial; consumer spending is the driving force of the economy; significant government spending is required for healthy economy; central economic planning by government is needed; central banking is required to manage the financial system which allows the payment of bills with cheap money. It is a system that has encouraged massively excessive credit card debt, student debt, consumer debt, corporate, mortgage, and government debt.

The long-term and short-term are not the same for all citizens. Some groups like today's middle-class are already very much aware of the onset of the major crisis. The full-fledged crisis which will engulf the world will be arriving in the not-too-distant future. It may not be a complete surprise for everyone, but nevertheless, it will still be shocking, dangerous, and obvious to everyone.

What Will the Crisis Look Like?

In the meantime, before liberty once again reasserts itself, what can we say about the coming conditions in the short- run? Another frequent question I get is: What will the huge political crisis look like? The simple answer is: chaos, economic turmoil, domestic violence, and multiple, worldwide military conflicts. Nothing pretty! The early signs are already present, with continuous and expanding conflicts in the Middle East in which we play a significant role.

The ongoing domestic violence we are now subject to results from class, cultural, and political power struggles. These conflicts will continue to increase in frequency and severity. Hate and violence have replaced Martin Luther King's peaceful civil disobedience as the means for bringing about change.

These social problems will turn into a crisis, but the government response, with further destruction of our civil liberties and the imposition of martial law, will be an even greater threat to our society. Under these conditions the American people may have to choose between civil war and chaos, both of which will be destructive to the principles of liberty. The "short- run" will need to run its course. The message of liberty will have to exert itself for it to solve the problems emanating from the illicit and arbitrary use of government force, which has wrongly interfered in the people's practice of voluntarism and consensual peaceful activity.

The shouting by the demagogues will be quite loud, blaming and agitating for political power and bailouts for special interests. Defending liberty, free markets, property ownership, and even the notion of peace will be constantly challenged. Newspeak will prevail. Truth will be rejected as language is destroyed.

The proponents of liberty will be ignored but never silenced, as they continue to offer the real solutions to the problems from which the world is suffering. Their efforts will only pay off after the "short-term" runs its course and the libertarian non-aggression approach is accepted. The sentiment and ideas that ushered in this ugly and dangerous worldwide crisis must be understood. Without that, a worthwhile solution is impossible.

Dealing with the gargantuan worldwide debt will plague the efforts of today's conventional economists. Accepting the notion that central bank creation of money is equivalent to wealth, or that it can facilitate wealth creation, will pose a great obstacle and prolong the suffering and delay the acceptance of free market principles.

Many principles accepted by our current political and educational leaders will be used to continue the bankrupt system. Here are some better principles that we should accept instead: 1) a right to life and liberty is not a right to someone else's stuff – even if obtained with the assistance of government force; 2) envy and greed must be rejected as a justified reason for government redistribution of wealth; 3) the wealthy who earn their own way are not to be judged in the same manner as those who became rich by using and benefiting government force; 4) intolerance of others for social or economic reasons, when violence is absent, must be rejected.

American society is already sharply divided, with most conflicts coming from the economic inequality generated by our system of central economic planning. This results from the policies of the Federal Reserve, the enormous number of regulations, and excessive taxation. Trying to solve the problem by forced redistribution and more of the same policies that we have been suffering from for decades will only make the violence and hatred between the haves and have-nots that much worse. Productivity is already sharply down and making it worse can't help.

Economic inequality, along with the destruction of the principles of liberty will be used as fodder for the Cultural

Marxists who continue to advocate violence as a solution to the chaos. For those who accept the principle of government violence to mold American society and the internal affairs of other nations, it's not much of a leap to increase the use of this principle of government violence to "pretend" they are now solving the inequities their policies created.

Though Cultural Marxism has been around for several decades, the failure of economic Marxism has prompted its leaders to promote their cause with this different strategy. Turmoil, conflict, and violence serves the interest of all supporters of authoritarianism who embrace a Marxist society.

Many of these participants are just plain evil. Some have difficulty handling unearned super wealth and are driven by guilt. This is combined with ignorance and stupidity. Hatred toward conservative social values and anything religious is evident on a daily basis. Using force to seek political power is characteristic of Marxist activists. Controlling the financial system is of greater concern to them than caring for the unfortunate. Much of their activities resemble the policies of the Jacobins during the French Revolution. Many millionaires and even billionaires promote this radical socio-economic philosophy. The failure of the current progressive system is the real culprit — a fact never discussed in the debates on how we got ourselves into this mess.

The migration crisis will continue to aggravate civil strife, not only in the United States but throughout the world. Migration and immigration per se is not the problem. The fact that the world migration disaster reflects a deeply flawed foreign policy, led by the United States and its allies, cannot be ignored. This problem needs resolved if we expect to keep civil disorder from getting totally out of control.

Immediately we ought to make it clear that there's no

easy road to citizenship. That would be the case especially for illegal immigrants. Our early tradition in dealing with immigrants required having either a sponsor or job before entering the United States. This policy should be reestablished. Concern for public health should also be part of the immigration process.

Preferential treatment for migrants is a source of great friction among Americans. Welfare is a deeply flawed system and the generous distribution of welfare to the influx of immigrants is a source of great anger. Many Americans are starting to realize that subsidizing migrants punishes Americans with higher taxes, loss of jobs, and social discord.

A more powerful, centrally controlled government, operating under authoritarian principles, is the most likely scenario once the violence gets out of control. This would essentially be martial law directed by the generals in charge of homeland security. Though total civil war is possible, hopefully we'll come to our senses by then and recognize the fallacies of progressivism and change our ways. Since the length of the short-term cannot be predicted, the tragic complications can continue for long periods of time, even years.

Over the past eight years, our society steadily has become more bifurcated, where 50 percent of the people are already in dire straits and the growing anger is only a hint of the things to come. This anger will last until a renewed respect for liberty occurs.

The government educational system, K through college, will become useless as the debt burden inundates its operation. The universities are already under control by professors and trustees who are obsessed with weird rules of political correctness and are culturally and racially biased. Total destruction of the First Amendment, except for themselves, is their goal.

Those responsible for how our universities are run are either clueless or deliberately destroying the economic and moral foundation of our society. Either way, the results are the same. The economic devastation, the cost of education, and the failure to fulfill its supposed purpose, will force those concerned to find an alternative to the steadily deteriorating college system.

Domestic "terrorism" will get much worse. Its perpetuation on US soil will continue to a greater extent by individuals born here rather than those foreign born and coming from the Middle East. Motivation for a terrorist act, however, will frequently relate to anger by some who claim sympathy for the victims of our destructive, terroristic foreign policy of killing tens of thousands of Muslims which we have been involved in for more than two decades.

The odds are great that the hatred that builds in a welfare state which guarantees benefits in response to immigrant demands for free stuff will lead to more political violence. The shooting at the Republican Party members of Congress baseball practice in Northern Virginia was clearly driven by hate and fearfulness that welfare benefits will not continue into the foreseeable future. This is not surprising since a bankruptcy of a country – which a major crisis signifies – makes it impossible for welfare benefits to continue forever. Hopefully we will never get as bad off as Venezuela, but our system has made us vulnerable to such a scenario. Violence related to changing the situation will have to run its course before it's realized that the Progressive Era is dead and gone and that liberty is accepted as the only solution to the chaos.

Equally important to the violence coming from the anger promoted by the politicians, the demagogues, and fear-mongers, will be the presence of wide-spread poverty.

Today, poverty is already a major concern, but the withering welfare system has been able to squeeze out enough token benefits to pacify, to some degree, the victims of the bad policies of economic interventionism.

But the time will come when the number of people living in poverty will dramatically increase, as the benefits dwindle, which will convert the crisis into a catastrophe. Think Venezuela! Hungry people, with little hope for the future, and political demagogues igniting the flames of hatred and victimhood with false promises, will set the stage for civil strife and destruction – a virtual social time bomb.

Those who are better off as a result of planning and preparation for bad times will be endangered by those who have accepted the entitlement philosophies and the politicians' promises. When the government fails in its efforts to print and spend its way out of the mess we're in, the people will take it into their own hands and carry out the "redistribution" to which they feel entitled.

The survivalists will be well armed with their preparation for the socioeconomic breakdown. Both sides will have guns. The philosophy of nonaggression and peaceful coexistence will be placed on the back burner, not for the long-term but until the libertarian revolution is successful.

How to Deal With the Crisis

What kind of plan should one have to deal with the coming crisis? The likelihood of chaos, domestic violence, increased poverty, and political infighting, will dominate once the crisis is underway. A major foreign war is likely to be going on as well. We will be more vulnerable due to our weakened position militarily and financially. As we descend from a preeminent position of power and wealth, our enemies, along with the resentment built up over the decades, will be much bolder at challenging us and will be more likely to turn against us as our position in the world is diminished.

The leaders of both political parties, the special interests, and the American people, are all influenced by Deep State fear-mongering, and will join in the struggle to stop a true revolution for liberty. The dangerous chaos will continue until our leaders endorse the notion that a free society must replace the authoritarians in charge. There's no reason to expect the powerful elite to peacefully walk away. Just surviving will be the chief motivation of most citizens.

The more there are who anticipated the breakdown of society and prepared themselves for it, the better. The struggle to survive and maintain reasonable security will occupy the attention of most citizens. Already we can see this effort going on in the Middle East countries ravaged by war and economic hardship. Just obtaining food, water, and shelter in the midst of these wars has precipitated one of history's greatest mass migrations, which is currently disrupting the stability of Europe. To some degree the same is happening here in the United States, and this will likely get worse as the economy continues to weaken. The Cultural Marxists are satisfied with the tragic crisis they help create. The decent people in the world are outraged.

Being prepared for such events – especially since there are uncertainties as to when they will occur – is far from easy. Some will do well as informed survivalists, with plans to have available emergency food, water, and shelter in a safe haven away from the more dangerous big cities. Many of our cities are already experiencing severe problems, like Detroit, Chicago, Baltimore, St. Louis, and many others. Along with the physical danger, there will be economic problems as a consequence of government dependency and debt run-up by municipalities and states. This will prevent an easy, temporary financial fix by increasing welfare benefits.

The rural safe havens that survivalists seek out will be available only to a few. This in itself makes the problems much worse and serves to aggravate class warfare between those who are doing well surviving, compared to those whose conditions deteriorate. Those who can plan for a special place, if things get out of hand, should. Those who can't must think of other options with the goal of avoiding violence if at all possible.

The most important thing is to know who your friends are and that you can trust them. Associating with like-minded people who understand the danger the government presents is crucial. A bankrupt government cannot finance the bribes and promises the people depend on. Many municipalities are already facing bankruptcies and will continue to depend on the federal government for a bailout. That will be self-limiting once the federal government debt limit is reached and basic needs for the people are not met. Merely printing up more currency will cease to work. A government that fails to provide the needed subsistence will not be able to provide police protection from the escalating violence. Seeking justice in the courts will be difficult. Government is already not trustworthy and the justice system is nothing more than gang warfare between political factions. This problem is destined to get worse. Security will become a responsibility of individuals and coalitions of people facing similar circumstances.

Building relationships within a group for self-defense will be discriminatory in aligning only with individuals that have similar social and political views. It will be necessary to identify and associate with those who reject the initiation of force as a means for survival. Under emergency conditions, governments will not be able to feed the hungry nor arrest the marauders stealing and looting for their own survival. Most of those who believe that our problems will lead to violence and that the government will not be able to help much will be armed to defend their families, their close allies, and their property.

The chaos may usher in an age of nullification of federal laws and this might be one of the unintended benefits of the Marxist-caused chaos. We already see that happening within the states, as some federal drug laws are being ignored. In a major crisis, this attitude could spread rather quickly to our benefit.

When people are forced to "survive on their own" without handouts from the government, they discover a tremendous incentive to be creative in caring for themselves. They become much more resourceful and efficient, as they are rewarded from personal effort rather than by lobbying Congress for free benefits. This will be something new for a lot of people and will prompt them to become creative and hopefully ambitious. Being responsible for one's own needs will be an education in itself.

When needs are provided by free people, acting in their own self-interest through peaceful means, it always outshines government bureaucratic inefficiency. Government programs can be temporarily helpful when the country is wealthy and still producing. But as people get poorer and more of them demand more free stuff from an already overwhelmed government, the benefits eventually come to an end.

Under these conditions it will be natural and beneficial

to get through the tough times by participating in the underground economy – which is actually the real economy. This has been done throughout history and is even occurring today in the United States. Those who are having trouble making ends meet frequently get involved in order to avoid excessive taxation and regulations. Wage and price controls in wartime and during rampant price inflation prompts black markets to immediately spring up. I remember the need for an underground economy during World War II, the Korean War, and in the Nixon era of the 1970's with wage and price controls. Prohibition of drugs and alcohol made the underground markets for these products prevalent and popular.

Most likely during a major crisis controls that inspire black markets should be expected. In a dollar crisis during bad economic times with massive debt, we can expect that the medium of exchange will have to be something of real value if the people lose confidence in the paper money. Silver and gold have been used throughout history under these circumstances. This phenomenon of a currency crisis creating serious economic and political problems is nothing new. Paper money may well be rejected by the people. Resorting to a crypto currency to serve as a substitute may occur. It obviously should be legal to do so, but I have my doubts about how effective it would be in tough times. That remains to be seen even though it is currently serving that purpose as a medium of exchange in the far East and in other parts of the world.

It will be more practical that items for daily living would be paid for in silver rather than gold due to the price differential. Gold could be used for larger purchases by some, but for daily living, silver would be a more practical option.

Individuals who are concerned about the possibility of a major economic crisis should be purchasing silver at the present time. Precious metals serve as a store of value and do not suffer the consequences suffered by many when fiat money totally collapses. The US has its own record of monetary debasement with destruction of the Continental dollar and the Confederate dollar. Our current dollar has been horrendously debased from a 1/20 of an ounce of gold at the time the Fed was established in 1913 to today when a dollar is defined as 1/1250 of an ounce of gold. In the crisis that I believe is coming, we'll see the ratio of both silver and gold to the dollar moving much higher. This means the purchasing power of gold and silver will skyrocket at the same time the paper money will continue to lose value. The more the people will have prepared for these events, the better off everyone will be.

During economic downturns, even when moderately severe like the one we've been experiencing since 2008, many believe that joining the military can best serve their interests. That is not a good idea. Our military will be used to contain violence and it's very likely that the military will be used to police the entire US population. It will be ugly and destabilizing for American young people to be shooting at other American young people who they may know and with whom they have no ax to grind. This happened during the rioting over the Vietnam War. In particular, the shooting of student protesters at Kent State University was a terrible blight on America and its military. It would be an untenable position to be put in if the military is called in to use force to perform domestic police actions. The real frustration, though, will be that many Americans will applaud the presence of the military if violence gets out of control. The best thing would be to steer clear of such a confrontation. That's when one should stay close to trusted friends and family for protection and survival.

Being able to provide private home education for children will be crucial. The government will likely see home and private schooling, which are telling the truth about the crisis, as subversive. The first amendment has already been severely undermined and freedom of speech will continue to be ruthlessly regulated on the Internet. This has already been happening. Progressives and other radical Cultural Marxists have gained the upper hand in our universities with the crazy notion of political correctness and unfortunately with minimal resistance from the people. Securing teaching materials before conditions totally deteriorate would be a wise move.

Even though all local police will not be corrupted, the culture of a militarized and aggressive police force will become more threatening to everyone. We will not be able to depend on the police protecting us from marauding groups. Of what value are the police even today in our large cities in maintaining peaceful conditions? The greater the crisis the less help the people can expect from the police. During hurricane Katrina, the police in New Orleans became more a part of the problem than helpful. The federal police operations under FEMA made a bad situation much worse.

Oath Keepers is a group asking all law enforcement personnel to take an oath that they would obey the law and the Constitution even if ordered to attack American citizens. The left considers this group to be radically un-American. They believe obedience to the state should drive everything the government does to provide safety and security for everyone.

The truth is that even in a free society economic security and personal safety depends on actions taken by law-abiding citizens, not by the police. In a time of a major crisis it becomes even more necessary for each individual to assume responsibility for their own safety.

In the midst of a major social and economic upheaval, our number one personal responsibility will remain the same as it has been for hundreds of years in the struggle to advance the cause of liberty: to reject all forms of authoritarianism. Allowing government officials to assume that they are exempt from telling the truth must cease. Conceding that the government can initiate violence to interfere with any peaceful activity must be rejected.

Whether now or in the midst of an overwhelming crisis, if we are to survive we must not forget that IDEAS are what ultimately makes the difference.

Promoting the moral defense of liberty and fully explaining why it is the only road to peace and prosperity must be continued under all conditions.

Rather than seeing the crisis as a disastrous end, we must see it as an opportunity to announce the death of 20th century Progressivism and America's military empire-building.

The door will be wide open, for practical economic and moral reasons, for believers in liberty to fill this void.

Just remember: even if it never gets as bad as some of us expect, the effort to promote the liberty message will never be wasted. That is what is needed today. It's too bad we can't deliver this message without a major economic upheaval, but it looks like that will not happen. Therefore, what we need today is a resurgence of belief in the morality and practicality of liberty. We need not wait until conditions deteriorate when it will be more difficult for us to spread the message.

The liberty message clearly provides the best chance to make the world more peaceful and prosperous. It's "an idea whose time has come." It is needed now more than ever.

Books mentioned in this book:

Omnipotent Government: The Rise of the Total State and Total War by Ludwig von Mises

For a New Liberty: The Libertarian Manifesto by Murray N. Rothbard

Notes on the State of Virginia by Thomas Jefferson

None Dare Call It Conspiracy by Gary Allen with Larry Abraham

The Economics of Liberty edited by Llewellyn H. Rockwell

The Foes of Our Own Household by Theodore Roosevelt

Nation, State and Economy: Contributions to the Politics and History of Our Time by Ludwig von Mises

Rules for Radicals by Saul D. Alinsky

My Larger Education, Being Chapters from My Experience by Booker T. Washington

On the Revolutions of Heavenly Spheres by Nicolaus Copernicus

Economics in One Lesson by Henry Hazlitt

CPSIA information can be obtained
at www.ICGtesting.com
Printed in the USA
LVOW12s2307191217
560334LV00003B/174/P